# FAITH
## —ON—
# FIRE

**BRANDON LEVI SPIKER**

# Faith of Fire

Brandon Levi Spiker
Email: bspiker@brandonspiker.org
www.brandonspiker.org

Cover Design: Roxie M Kirk
Editor: Richard Smith
Consultant: HOV Publishing
Contact the Author: Brandon Levi Spiker bspiker@brandonspiker.org

For further information regarding special discounts on bulk purchases, please contact:
Brandon Levi Spiker at bspiker@brandonspiker.org

ISBN Paperback:  979-8-9887220-0-7
ISBN Hardcase:   979-8-9887220-1-4
ISBN eBook:      979-8-9887220-2-1

Printed in the United States of America

# Dedication

This book is dedicated to the memory of Bishop Bill Godair. He was a remarkable man whose unwavering dedication to his faith and community touched the lives of countless individuals. Not only was Bishop Godair a spiritual leader, but he was also a mentor and friend to many. His leadership and guidance were instrumental in shaping the lives of those around him, including Tara and me. We will always be grateful for the opportunity he provided us to embark on this journey as Pastors of Cornerstone Church. The legacy of Bishop Godair will live on in the hearts of everyone he inspired with his larger-than-life personality. We are honored to dedicate this book to him and express our deepest gratitude for his impact on our lives. Thank you. Your presence will always be felt in our hearts and minds. We love you and will see you on the other side!

# Acknowledgements

First and foremost, I give all the glory and honor to my Lord and Savior, Jesus Christ, who has been my constant source of inspiration, strength, and guidance throughout my life. Without His grace and mercy, this book would not have been possible. I would also like to express my heartfelt gratitude to the following individuals who have played a significant role in bringing this book to life:

To Pastor Tina Godair, thank you for entrusting us with this assignment and for your unwavering support, guidance, and love. Your faith in our abilities has been a constant source of inspiration and motivation.

To Sensei Ricky Smith, thank you for your tireless effort, dedication, and countless hours spent working with me on this book. Your insight and expertise have been invaluable in shaping this project.

To my Cornerstone Church family, thank you for your prayers, encouragement, and unwavering support throughout this journey. Your love, support, and grace have motivated me to reach higher and believe God for greater.

I am also profoundly grateful to my mother, Carlene, for her unconditional love and support throughout my life. I love you, Mom.

And last but not least, I would like to express my deepest gratitude to my wife, Tara, the love of my life, for her unwavering love and commitment to our family and the call of God on our lives. Your love, support, and sacrifice allow me to pursue my dreams and passions. I love you with all my heart Tara. To my son, Isaac, and my daughter, Gracie, Daddy loves you.

# Table of Contents

# Foreword

It is with great appreciation for my Pastor, Brandon Levi Spiker, that I write this foreword. Not only is he my pastor, I am his Sensei. He is one of my karate students, along with his son, Isaac. For me, it is an honor to be the Sensei of my Pastor, who also happens to be a Black Belt. Because of this unique blessing, we have developed an invaluable friendship of love and respect.

A highlight for me every week is sitting under the anointed teaching of Pastor Brandon during his Wednesday night Bible Study. He has such a gift of presenting God's Word in a simple but powerful way that brings spiritual insight to the Word of God. He has a deep passion and commitment to lift everyone out of their comfort zone, inspiring them to operate in a higher dimension of faith so they can receive what God's Word has promised for their life.

*Faith on Fire* will challenge any reader's walk in faith. This is not just a religious feel-good book. This book will compel readers to search their hearts and transform their thinking, authorizing them to live at their fullest potential of what God has called them to be. So many Christians today are walking in defeat because they do not understand who they are and the rights they possess as a believer. In this book, Pastor not only teaches, but he ministers to the heart of the reader. He makes it clear that anyone can embark on this journey of faith, elevating their belief system to a greater level.

His ministry experience preaching in eighteen countries around the world has blessed him with insight and knowledge that is almost incomprehensible, except for the fact that the faith of God is working in and through him. It is evident that Pastor Spiker is equipped with all the gifts of the five-fold ministry. His vision is that everyone reading this book will catch revelation knowledge in their heart, setting their spirit on fire with faith!

Sensei Ricky Smith

# Preface

Faith is a powerful force that has shaped the lives of many people throughout history. Faith has inspired individuals to receive great things from God. By faith, people have overcome seemingly insurmountable obstacles. Through faith, people have discovered hope and meaning in the face of adversity.

Yet, for many of us, faith can be a source of confusion, doubt, and even despair. We struggle to understand what it means to have faith, how to cultivate it, and how to apply it in our daily lives. It is precisely these challenges that are addressed in this book, *Faith on Fire*.

*Faith on Fire* will help you discover insights and practical views on faith that will deepen your understanding and enable you to walk in your God-given potential. Drawing on a wealth of wisdom and revelation from God's Word, this book offers a unique and compelling perspective on faith that is both enlightening and empowering.

Whether you are a seasoned believer or a curious seeker, *Faith on Fire* will help you explore the many dimensions of faith and discover new ways of cultivating and expressing it. Join me in this journey of discovery as we explore the mysteries and wonders of faith together. May this book be a source of inspiration and guidance to all who are seeking to kindle their own faith on fire!

Pastor Brandon Levi Spiker

# Introduction

Have you ever wondered why people go through specific struggles in their life? Are these struggles by happenchance? Do some people draw the short straw in life while others seem to sail right through it with all the luck? What if you could actually have a say in altering the course of circumstances in your life? What if it was possible to turn your situation around? Can you actually transform a lifestyle of turmoil and depression to a lifestyle of peace and joy, a lifestyle of barely getting by to a lifestyle of prosperity, or a lifestyle of unhealthiness to a lifestyle of health?

Yes, you can! How do I know? Because the living God who spoke the heavens and earth into existence declared through His Word that we have the authority. But we have to have faith in God's Word. In order to have this faith, we must examine our own belief system and have a good understanding of what it is that we actually believe. When searching for hope, do we put our trust in the world system, or do we place our trust in the loving God who created us?

What exactly is faith, and how do we develop it? In this book, we will learn that faith is a powerful spiritual force that can be developed and put into action so that we can receive the promises of God's Word. Is there a difference between fact and truth? Can truth change fact? How can we develop our faith to a level that makes the impossible possible? Is faith a gift? Can anyone possess faith? Is there a measure of faith that some have, and others do not? These are some of the questions that I will address.

You will learn the key to unlocking your faith. You will learn the source of your faith. You will also learn the source of fear, which is the spiritual force that works against faith. I will share six major hindrances that can hinder your faith. Is there an enemy of God who can rob our faith? Can sin keep us from obtaining faith? What exactly is sin, and how can we overcome it? How can we become righteous enough to walk in faith and get results?

When does faith happen? How long does it take to receive something you desire from God? How long does it take to develop or grow your faith? Can we develop faith on our own? We will discuss the adjustments we must make to obtain the most significant dimension of faith. There are specific actions that God commands us to do to possess our heart's desires. But first, we must get our hearts right to operate in the God-like kind of faith.

Who owns the earth? Who has authority over it? We have learned things about faith that we must unlearn. We must get our old thinking out of the way. When making decisions, can we trust our feelings and emotions? Does having faith require us to fight? What kind of fight? Where is the battle? How can we win?

I have dedicated my life to teaching people how to overcome any circumstance by walking in genuine Bible faith. I have witnessed countless individuals who chose to live by faith and receive the blessings that God has for them. I am a testimony of how God can launch you from living in poverty to experiencing abundantly above what you could ever imagine.

In this book, I will give you a sure formula to continue increasing your faith to another level. You might think that you do not qualify; you are not good enough; you were not born with what it takes, but that is not true. It would help if you simply learned how to have faith in your faith. The pages of this book hold the ticket to obtaining victory in every area of your life. The missing link to your success will be revealed. As you read this book, your spirit will begin to catch supernatural insight that will ignite your faith.

My heart desires that this book, *Faith on Fire,* reveals how to see yourself as God sees you. I genuinely believe that you will learn to overcome any obstacles that are robbing you of walking in the abundant life that God has promised in His Word. Not only will you learn how to walk in faith constantly, but also how to elevate your faith to receive the things you desire in life. It is not an accident that you are reading this book; it is part of God's divine plan. You must never give up. You have to put your foot down and begin to declare what is rightfully yours! It is time to set your *Faith on Fire*!

# CHAPTER 1

## *Faith on Fire:*
## The Substance of What is Desired

What is faith? Hebrews 10:23 declares, *Let us hold fast the profession of our faith without wavering; (for he is faithful that promised).* But first, we must understand faith. What exactly is faith? Faith is simply the substance of what is desired. Hebrews 10:34 states, *For ye had compassion of me in my bonds, and took joyfully the spoiling of your goods, knowing in yourselves that ye have in heaven a better and an enduring substance.* Faith is the substance of heaven on the inside of us. Anything connected to your faith is the substance of what God has instilled in you from a heavenly realm. What is faith? Hebrews 11:1 says, *Now faith is the substance of things hoped for, the evidence of things not seen.*

Now faith is the heavenly substance of what we desire in our hearts. It is the heavenly part of us or the divine nature of God on the inside of us. Hebrews 11:3 says that the world was framed by faith. God operates in the realm of faith, so when we operate in faith, we operate out of the substance of the divine nature of who God is. The Bible says that we were created in the image of God. When we operate in faith, we are not operating out of our flesh or carnality; we are operating out of the heavenly realm. You must stop rehearsing what you *don't* desire because, remember, the substance of what you are experiencing is what you have desired or spoken in your heart. Now, let me explain.

## Carnality vs. Faith

We are a spirit, we live in a body, and we have a soul. When we talk about a body, we are talking about three different rooms of a house. Even though a house has three rooms, it is still only one house. You are a spirit, you live in a body, and you have a soul. Even though I am a spirit, I am in a body, and I have a soul. That does not make me three separate people. It makes me one person. For instance, I am a husband to my wife Tara, a son to my mother Carlene, and a father to my son Isaac. Those are titles and not who I really am. At the end of the day, my name is Brandon.

You have to understand that when you were created, you were created with a spirit, but you also have a soul which has not yet been converted. When you are saved and baptized, your spirit is saved. According to the Scripture, this body obviously will one day put on immortality. That is why we say salvation is a progression because it is the conversion of the soul. The word soul comes from the word *saku*, which we get the word *psyche*, which refers to your mind, will, intellect, and emotions. The soul is converted over the process of time by renewing your mind with the Word of God. Until your soul is converted, you deal with this little thing called carnality.

When you start rehearsing what you *don't* desire to God, preachers, counselors, family, or your spouse, you are not operating out of your faith but out of your carnality. God does not respond to carnality; he does not even respond to need; he responds to faith. When you read the Gospels, Jesus always said, "It is by your faith that you have been made whole." It is by your faith that you receive everything that God wants you to have. The problem is that we must learn the difference between praying out of carnality and praying in faith.

2

## Walking in the Past

Rehearsing what you *don't* desire is rehearsing your past mistakes. It is really hard to walk in faith when you are still telling people about the mistakes you made years ago. The enemy can trick you into living in this little box by looking at what you have done in the past as being humble. It is easy to fall into this trap. But it takes faith to know that Jesus Christ has forgiven us of our past mistakes. Praise God!

We tell people that God forgives us, but can we receive that truth for ourselves? Can we let go of the things that we have done in the past? The enemy's strategy is to keep us in the past. We are so focused on something we did yesterday that we cannot see the future God has for us. We cannot see where we are going. We cannot see what we are believing for our kids, our spouse, our family, or our job situation. We cannot see the breakthrough that is coming because we are too focused on repeating something that happened in the past. The enemy says, "Look what you did." You cannot operate in faith for the *now* if you're living in the past. You can't walk in faith today living in yesterday.

## Sin vs. Righteousness

People continue to live in sin because they have a sin conscious. The reason they are sin conscious is because, in their mind, the devil is constantly reminding them of their carnality. Many times it has nothing to do with the devil; it has everything to do with you. Sometimes I think the devil stands before the Lord and says, "God, I promise I didn't do it this time. It wasn't me. It was their carnality; they were acting crazy." It is easy for people to blame the devil to justify living in sin. They rehearse and stay where they are, blaming everything on the devil to justify who they are. No, they had some say in it. What they have to do is take some responsibility and say, "God,

3

I did this. I need your fire to come in and burn it out of me because it really didn't have anything to do with the devil. It had everything to do with the carnality in my mind."

When you are sin conscious, you will always produce sin in your life because you are rehearsing sin. But the minute you become righteous conscious, you start acting righteous and rehearsing righteousness. Before you can be righteous, you have to believe that you are in right standing with God through Jesus Christ. Corinthians 5:21 states, *For he hath made him to be sin for us, who knew no sin; that we might be made the righteousness of God in him.* Do you still believe you are a sinner? Some say, "Well, we're just a sinner saved by grace." Actually, that is not true; it is not even biblical to say it. You *were* a sinner, but you have been saved by grace, and now you are called the righteousness of God in Christ Jesus. Once you start desiring righteousness, it will manifest out of you and become your substance in life.

## Watch Your Language

When you truly start walking a lifestyle of faith, you will pay attention to your vocabulary. For example, when people say, "That's way too expensive." Here is another way to say it. "I don't choose to allocate the funds in that direction." It just takes a slight adjustment in your confession to speak the mindset of faith on a higher level. I am not talking about being super spiritual and praying about whether you should eat Fruity Pebbles or Cocoa Puffs. But, I am saying that you should examine your speech. Is it lining up with the person of faith that you are? Does your speech confirm your belief that you have been born again, you are the righteousness of God, and He desires to bless you? Does your vocabulary, the words coming out of your mouth, and the statements you tell your kids and grandkids align with everything you believe? Because every single word that we speak plants a seed in our mind.

My wife used an example of her vocabulary when we were selling our house. She believed God and confessed that it would appraise at a certain amount. She was saying, "In the name of Jesus, our house will appraise for this amount." Then she caught herself using the "if" word a few times, which opened the door of doubt in her mind. She would say to herself, "Tara, don't you say that. The house is going to appraise for the exact amount I believe, in Jesus' name." And don't you know, Praise God, it did! When you are focused on the substance of what you desire, you will quickly make the necessary adjustments to your vocabulary to align with the result.

We have to be very careful not to backtrack what we are believing by planting bad seeds in our minds with the words we speak. We will begin to believe it in our hearts, and what is in our hearts will come out of our mouths.

Luke 6:45 says:

A good man out of the good treasure of his heart bringeth forth that which is good; and an evil man out of the evil treasure of his heart bringeth forth that which is evil: for of the abundance of the heart his mouth speaketh. (KJV)

If you hear yourself saying something that is not faith, you must go back and say, "Search me, God; show me what's in my heart. Do I truly believe that you want to bless me? Why am I speaking this way? If there is anything in my heart not of you, Lord, get it out. I am only going to speak in faith."

To put this in perspective, having faith and speaking the opposite is not denying what you are going through. You are not denying the doctor's diagnosis; you are just choosing to believe the report of the Lord over the diagnosis. I am not saying that you should lie and say, "Oh, I don't have a cold today," when your nose is running, and you have a fever. If you are not careful, you can get real flakey with this and find yourself in the granola section of the grocery store, you know, with the rest of the fruits, flakes, and nuts. I am not saying to operate in denial, but to make sure you are not receiving anything not of God and that you are returning it to the sender, the devil. Just because it is sent does not mean you have to sign for the package. Send it back to hell from whence it came. How do you do that? You do it with your words. You are not denying what you have, but you are saying with your words, "No, this is not my portion. I might be going through this in the natural realm, but I am in the heavenly realm, and this is only temporary and not the end result because the word has already declared the opposite for my life. So, I choose to speak the word over anything else because the word prevails." If you work the word, the word will work for you.

Let's apply this to prosperity. Excelling in something desired is the true definition of prosperity. You have stepped into a realm of prosperity when you excel in what you desire. Prosperity is not just about money, although money is included. The definition of prosperity that the Lord gave me a long time ago is *nothing missing, nothing out of place*. How many of you have some things that are missing? Is your money lacking? Is your health lacking? When we start excelling, we believe by faith that we are in good health. When we start excelling in what we desire, we begin to confess it; we begin to practice it; we begin to walk in it, and that is when we start experiencing the manifestation of what we have desired, which means that we have stepped into a new realm of prosperity for our life.

## Come on Now

What is faith? Now faith is! If it is *not* now, it is *not* faith. If you are not healed now, it is not faith. If you are not blessed now, it is not faith. That is why when we say, "I believe that it will come," it is not coming because it is not now. Revival is not coming; revival is here. Revival broke out in the second chapter of Acts and never stopped; we just stopped looking for it. It never left. The heavens never closed. They were opened when Jesus was baptized in the water. They were opened, and they never closed. And by the way, the Holy Ghost isn't a bird either. So the heavens open everything. Everything you are believing God for has already been given, and it is here right now! Do you have the revelation that enables you to receive it right now?

Here is a good example of how faith operates in the now! If my son would ask his mother for ice cream, "Mommy, I want some ice cream." And she said, "Yes, Isaac, we will go get you some ice cream." Getting from the house to the grocery store would take some time. If he continually asked for ice cream all the way to the grocery store, because he could probably ask a good thirty times in that timeframe, he would be operating in disbelief and annoying his mother. But if he just said, "Wow, thank you for getting me ice cream, Mommy." He believed it because she said it. He believed that she would fulfill her promise instead of continually asking. There is a time difference between when she said yes and how long it took before Isaac ate his ice cream.

There are times when God will say yes, and you do not see it at that exact moment. But He is working it out. It is already there; it is laid up for you. He is just taking you from the house to the grocery store in that car. We should just praise Him all the way to the store and enjoy the ride. The Lord is our provider. There have been times when someone did not pay us, and I could have responded by saying, "They

7

forgot to pay us." But instead, I would say, "Well, they can't steal it from me because I have already given it to them." If they are holding on to it, they need it more than I do, so they can have it. That is a seed because everything in life is a seed sown. The Lord will always provide for me. No one can take anything from me because I am willing to give it all away. Yes, everything; the car, the house, and the money. They can take it all because I am sowing it all. My life is a seed. If I plant it, God is going to grow it and give me something bigger and better. He has every time!

## Who is Faith?

Hebrews 11:6 says, *But without faith it is impossible to please him: for he that cometh to God must believe that he is, and that he is a rewarder of them that diligently seek him.* That *He is* what? *He is* God. The God of your life is the creator of heaven and earth, the one who gives the blessings. *He is*, and *He is* a rewarder. If you have faith which is the substance of what you desire, you are pleasing God. If you believe that *He is* God and that He wants to reward you because you are diligently seeking Him, God will do what He has promised. That is who He is.

Faith does not have to know *how*, but it has to know *who*. Most of us want a blueprint of how the things we are believing for are going to happen. God, just send it on down; I'd like to see it all and know every twist and turn of exactly how it is going to happen. But that would take zero faith. If you think about it, we have everyday faith in things we don't even realize we have faith in. Most of us get in the car and go to work every day. We don't know exactly how the car operates, but we have faith that the car is going to get us from point A to point B. You hear success stories about someone who had a mom-and-pop shop that exploded with success overnight. It just happened. They kept doing the right thing, and one day it exploded. Sometimes we are trying to have more faith when we merely need to focus on God and let it happen. We simply need to listen to the Holy Spirit.

Faith in God is saying, "God, I have no idea how this business is going to explode. I have no idea how this ministry is going to explode, but I trust you and believe it." Even if He gives you a blueprint, lays the whole thing out for you, speaks directly to you, and tells you exactly how to do it, it will still take major faith to implement it. I have never seen God give anyone a plan that is attainable in their own strength. Never have I seen Him say, "You know what, go ahead and do this, and it will be the easiest thing you have ever done, and I am just going to open the floodgates of heaven and bless you more than you have ever been blessed." No, because he is building your character when you are walking through something that seems impossible. He is building up something on the inside of you that is rising and growing. Then you will have a testimony to share when you get there. But if it were easy, you would not experience the growth. If someone just gave you a billion dollars today, that's a blessing, right? But what does that teach you? The things that are cultivated inside of us that we can pass on for generations are what God does for us; that is how he strengthens us.

You may not even realize it, but your carnality may allow you to have faith in certain people and things, and you will actually find yourself serving that person or thing more than God. You have to be totally reliant on God and have your faith in Him. What if you lost your job or income source tomorrow? You didn't realize your faith was in your job because you regularly got the same paycheck. So you were just naturally reliant on that income without having to believe God for anything. But if everything was taken away from you tomorrow, do you have enough faith to sustain you and believe God will take care of you?

You cannot put your faith in your job, your boss, a family member, or anything else. Your faith has to be utterly reliant on the Holy Ghost. It cannot be reliant on anyone or anything but the Lord. You have to trust God in every area of your life completely. You may not know what is going to happen tomorrow, but you still have to have faith. God forbid this ever happen, but what if all the grocery stores shut down tomorrow? You want to talk about chaos. Even worse, what if the banks shut down? You would see this place turn upside down in a New York second. If all your money was suddenly gone, are you going to panic? Or are you going to trust the Lord? You cannot put your faith and trust in anything but the Lord. Rely on Him. Your job is not your source; the Lord is your source. He is your source of provision. He is your way maker. The Lord wants us to rely on Him solely.

## God Pleasures in our Desires

Psalm 35:27 says, *Let them shout for joy, and be glad, that favour my righteous cause: yea, let them say continually, Let the LORD be magnified, which hath pleasure in the prosperity of his servant.* God takes pleasure in prospering His servant. The things that He has provided for His servant, they have according to the substance of their faith. So God is saying if you desire it, I take pleasure in giving it to you. That is why we must desire miracles, signs, and wonders with all of our hearts. That is why we have to desire things, not just for ourselves but for other people to receive, such as salary raises, increases in business, new homes, new cars, new jobs, and debt cancellation. Because the more we desire it and speak it, the more substance there will be from our faith.

And get this. God takes pleasure when we have received what He has provided. Everything that you believed God for has already been provided. Okay, what do you mean? When God created the Earth, He created everything in a divine order. He created the water before He created the fish because He knew that the water would be the provision for the fish. God created your provision and what you desire in this life before you were even in your mother's womb. He created it because He needed to ensure there would be more than enough for you and your family before you ever popped up on the scene. Accident or no accident, He already had it created.

## Speak What We Desire

And when you go through difficulties and challenges, if you allow faith to kick in, you will use the challenge as a notification to let your mind know that what you need is already on the way.

Mark 11:22-24 declares:

And Jesus answering saith unto them, Have faith in God. For verily I say unto you, That whosoever shall say unto this mountain, Be thou removed, and be thou cast into the sea; and shall not doubt in his heart, but shall believe that those things which he saith shall come to pass; he shall have whatsoever he saith. Therefore I say unto you, What things soever ye desire, when ye pray, believe that ye receive them, and ye shall have them. (KJV)

All things that we do not desire have to be taken out. All doubt has to be removed. We have to speak aloud what we desire. We can desire it all day, but we must say it out of our mouths to receive it. He shall have whatever he says. You have to speak it into the atmosphere. So when you desire it, then you pray. When you pray, do not beg. Intercession is not begging. Remember, if your provision or desire was created before you, all you have to do is thank Him for it... in His name. Believe that you shall receive. So when you thank Him for it, you have to believe it at the very moment you are receiving it. You must believe that you are receiving at the same time you are asking. Faith is now. I have to

11

believe right now all my debt is paid. Right now, depression is leaving my mind. Right now, sickness is leaving my body. Faith operates in the now.

We were in a meeting the other day, and I observed a person asking someone to do something with the assumption that they were already going to do it. I thought, "Man, I need to start doing that." She knows how to get things done. That is how we should be with our faith. We should assume God is already going to take care of it and that the devil has been defeated!

Mark 4:39 says, *And he arose, and rebuked the wind, and said unto the sea, Peace, be still. And the wind ceased, and there was a great calm.* We have to speak the desired end results. Whatever results you want, you have to speak it. You have to speak it out of your mouth and be specific about it. You have to get specific with what you want God to do in your life.

Luke 17:5-6 states:

And the apostles said unto the Lord, Increase our faith. And the Lord said, If ye had faith as a grain of mustard seed, ye might say unto this sycamine tree, Be thou plucked up by the root, and be thou planted in the sea; and it should obey you. (KJV)

It just takes some faith. Some of you are thinking that you will look like a goofball. It doesn't matter what people think. Anytime God calls you to do something great, you are always going to look foolish in the natural. You have to speak the desired end result. When your car is having trouble, you had better speak to it. When things are crazy at home, you better draw a line in the sand and say, "No, I'm laying down the law; I am a child of God in the family of faith. I am not allowing

12

confusion to tear our home apart. There is peace in my home in the name of Jesus."

You have to exercise your authority over it. God declared in the first chapter of His Word that He created man in His own image and gave him dominion over the Earth. The word dominion means title, deed, or ownership. When you are the owner of land, you have the authority to control the outcome of what is happening to it. You have to confess it. You have to declare, "I am more than a conqueror; I am the head, not the tail; I am above and not beneath; I am healed; I am whole; I am restored, even when I don't feel it in this natural body. I do not go by my feelings, I do not go by my emotions, but I go by what has been declared by the Word. I am who God says I am. I am blessed in the city; I am blessed in the field; I am blessed going in; I am blessed going out, and everything I put my hands to is blessed. That is who I am because that is who He created me to be. You have to confess, "I am." You have to confess, "I can." When you confess, "I can," you are releasing God's ability within you to do all things through Christ who strengthens you. "Yes, I can be wealthy; yes, I can walk in prosperity; yes, I can be healed; yes, I am healed." You have to speak it. Yes, you *can*, and yes, you *will*. Whatever the word says is what I can do.

Now catch this in your spirit; confession brings possession. Jesus is the promise. Everything attached to Him has already been granted to you. It is in our new birth experience, what we have in Jesus, what Jesus is doing in us now, and what God is doing through us. You have to confess it if you want to possess it. What do you want to possess? What do you desire? Faith in God is the substance of what you desire. Faith is simply the substance of what is desired. God wants to set your faith on fire with the substance of what you desire!

# CHAPTER 2

## Faith on Fire:
## Developing Your Faith

How do we develop our faith? When you study faith, if you are not careful, many things will become redundant to you. And the minute it starts to get old, that is an indication that you do not yet have the revelation of faith. The Bible says in Romans 10:17, *So then faith cometh by hearing, and hearing by the word of God.* Faith comes by what? Faith comes by hearing the Word of God. The more you hear the Word, the more revelation knowledge will begin to rise in you. You can hear the same Scripture repeatedly; however, you will get a new revelation every time.

Hebrew 12:1-2 states:

Wherefore seeing we also are compassed about with so great a cloud of witnesses, let us lay aside every weight, and the sin which doth so easily beset us, and let us run with patience the race that is set before us, Looking unto Jesus the author and finisher of our faith; who for the joy that was set before him endured the cross, despising the shame, and is set down at the right hand of the throne of God. (KJV)

When people hear the word *sin*, they think of sipping, cussing, and dipping. That is the usual impression of sin. But the Bible refers to sin as anything in your life that causes you to miss the mark or anything that keeps you from fulfilling your purpose in life. Sin is any barrier that causes you to delay or stop fulfilling your purpose or walk in God.

So anything can become a sin if it is causing you to live a life of procrastination. It is not that the *action* is sin; it is that you make it sin. You make it sin when it becomes a god in your life.

Hebrews 12:2 refers to the right hand of the throne of God. People interpret the "right hand of God" as a person sitting in the center of the throne and someone sitting on the right-hand side of them. That is actually a misinterpretation or misconception of what is taking place. Any time the Word refers to a right hand, it refers to the scepter that a king would rule with in his kingdom. "Right hand of God" refers to the scepter or the ruling of a king. It is not describing a separate individual. It is talking about the scepter that the king rules with; it is the right hand of power. His scepter is literally in his right hand on the throne of God, which is His ability to rule or declare something in your life or in the earth.

To develop our faith, we must understand that according to Hebrews 12:2, Jesus is, in reality, the developer of our faith. He is the author and the finisher of it. The deeper the revelation we have in Jesus, the deeper level of faith we will be able to walk and operate in to receive what God has for our life. What we really have to do is receive Jesus as the developer of our faith and understand what the Word is. John 1:14 explains, *"Jesus was the word made flesh."* The Word is Jesus. The more I get the Word on the inside of me, the more my faith is developed. The more you get the Word on the inside of you, the more you get Jesus in you. The more you get a revelation of Him, the more you understand Him. Then you will begin to understand that He is the author and the finisher, the beginning and the end, and everything in between. There is nothing outside of Christ. In Him is everything. So we have to get a revelation of who Christ is. As we begin to receive a revelation of who He is, we begin to have confidence in His ability to do miracles, signs, and wonders in our lives. Faith and confidence are one and the same.

16

If you have confidence — fully relying on Jesus and putting that trust in Him on the line when you believe God for something, He will develop your faith to receive what you are asking for. The more you use your faith, the more your faith increases. Faith not only comes from God's Word, but it grows by God's Word. Without a continuous intake of the Word of God, your faith will stop growing. When you accepted Christ into your heart and were baptized in His name, it was not the end; it was the beginning of the revelation of Christ. A deeper revelation of Him will begin to unfold in increments. If God revealed everything to us at one time, we could not handle it. When the God of the heavens touches us in a profound way, it is a miracle that we can even survive it. God feeds us pieces so we can grow and mature as we increase in faith. But the only way to get more of Him is to get more of the Word on the inside of us. In order to do that, we have to have a constant intake of the Word of God in our life.

If you tell an unbeliever to have faith, what should they have faith in? When we are believing for something, we can begin to make an idol out of what we are believing for, because we become consumed with it. But when we get consumed with the developer of our faith, what we are believing for becomes easier because our mind is not consumed with it. So, if we tell an unbeliever to have faith, we have to tell them who to have faith in. It is Jesus, the developer of our faith. Just have faith in Jesus!

## A Revelation

When Elijah defeats the Prophets of Baal in 1 Kings 18:19-29, he says, *The God of Abraham, Isaac, and Israel.* He recognized who God was. We have to apply who God is in our situation to have faith. Otherwise, what do we have faith in? We are just blowing to and fro with the wind. If we are captivated by His glory, His goodness, His grace, and His mercy, knowing that we are His child and we are about His business, we can have faith because we are called to get things done. We have a kingdom purpose; we have a mission; we have an assignment, and it is all for His glory. We are on a mission, we know that we are called, and we know we are a child of God; therefore, we can speak with confidence. If not, we are just believing for something, and that is all we think about. If we are captivated by Jesus, He will take care of us.

Many believers in churches do not earnestly know who Jesus Christ is. They do not have a revelation of Him. Their relationship is through another person's relationship. They do not have a personal relationship on their own with him. They have never met their maker; they have never received Him; they have never had an encounter with God. Therefore, their relationship with God is through their pastor, preacher, mother, or grandma, and they only go by what they have been told about who He is. They never find out, for themselves, who He truly is. They have learned the behavior of Christianism. They have mastered how to sing and shout about Him. Matthew 15:8 says, *You tell people about me with your lips, but your heart is far from me.* You have to have an encounter with God yourself. You have to know who He is. He was your grandmother's savior, but is He also your savior? Is He your redeemer? Is He your way maker? You have heard about Him healing everybody else, but have you given Him the opportunity to give you a miracle and be a way maker for you?

We have a lot of people that are shouting based on somebody else's relationship. We feel all the hype and all the goosebumps and think that it is a move of God, but a move of God is when you get a revelation of who He really is in your life. When you get a revelation of who Jesus is and what He has done for you, nothing will hold you down or cause you to run with your tail tucked between your legs. When you get a revelation of who Jesus is, you get saved for real!

18

I had a relationship with the Lord, and I am not disqualifying my early years, but in 2009 I was going through a mental crisis. I was just burned out. I had preached three hundred meetings that year and was completely exhausted. I was almost at the point of a nervous breakdown. After that, I quit traveling for about a month; I was done. I was done with church folk and everything. I ended up feeling better and doing many other things when the Lord spoke to me and told me to do a series of meetings. At first, I was hesitant and fought it. I was still hearing God and just going by faith because I wasn't feeling anything.

The first night of the conference was packed out; God moved in a powerful way, and the entire revival turned into weeks, with every single night filled to capacity. People were showing up two hours early to get into the building. That Monday night, I literally had a vision in the service. I saw this figure in a robe before me, with shining beams of light behind him. Every time he moved, the garments on him would change colors like a rainbow. People might think I'm crazy or out of my mind, but I'm not; I'm just out of their minds. This figure reached his hand out to me, and my flesh was pulling away. But it was like my flesh was fighting. I was trembling and scared to death. When people claim they saw an angel, or they saw Jesus, I'm like, if you really saw Him, you are not going to be just sitting there saying, "Hey, nice to see you."

You are going to be scared. If Jesus Christ walked into the room where you are, none of you would be standing around talking to Him. You would be shaking with the fear of the Lord. You would be scared for your life because you are so close to eternity that you can't conceive it. I was scared to death; I knew I was about to die. But the spirit of God within me kept pushing me forward. And when I grabbed his hand, He stepped in on the inside of me. When He stepped in on the inside of me, I was literally shaking for two days straight. I didn't fall on the ground, get back up twenty seconds later, and walk out the same way I came in. I shook for two days under the power of God. They had to carry me out of that service. I was shaking in the car all the way home. I lay in my bed and shook all night. I couldn't do anything. The following day I was still shaking but had my bearings. I opened to Revelation 4:3 and read the Scripture that explained, *His garments are like rainbows, he who sits on the throne.* I knew I had an encounter with Jesus! When I had that encounter with Him, I knew who He was, and God instantly downloaded revelation knowledge in me that no one could teach me. Because some things can't be taught, they can only be caught.

## A Close Encounter

This is the answer to our problems. We need to get a revelation of Christ and have encounters with Him. We never make that leap of faith because we worry about what other people think. When you read the Book of Acts, they underwent some radical experiences. Many people have created the mindset that radical experiences died with the early church. The church never died. The Book of Acts is still being written today. We as a church have to get hungry for the demonstration of God's power — real signs, wonders, and miracles. We cannot put this into a certain "Oh, those people are crazy" mentality.

I have no reputation; it is His reputation. The minute you stop worrying about what other people think, the second you get out of your mind and in your spirit, you will start hungering and thirsting after His righteousness. When you encounter God, things will radically change in your life, and you will never go back to certain things. One of those things is fear. You will never go back to fear. You will never worry about anything again. You will think, "Now that I have met Him, I already know what heaven is like." But we have to get hungry and thirsty for that. Our faith has to be developed for that. We have to get a revelation of Him.

When you have an encounter with Him, you cannot live life normally afterward. When my wife got saved, she didn't have a church community. She was twenty years old and was sitting in a church, and a lady said, "If you would like to speak in tongues, come down here." She didn't know what tongues were. She had read about it in the Bible but didn't fully understand it. She thought, "I'm not going up there." My wife is not the kind of person who likes to be in front of people. She explains how she was just sitting there, and it was as if liquid fire came on her. She began to shake. It was like lightning bolts hit her, and she just started speaking in tongues.

She continued to go back to this lady's meetings. The lady was a prophet and would prophesy over her every night. She did not have an open vision or anything like that, but that touch of God made her hungry for Him. When you get saved, all you know is the world's way. And then you enter into an environment like this, and you feel the love of believers. This was different than anything my wife had ever experienced. Sickness was no longer her daily bread. Poverty was no longer her daily bread. She kept returning to those meetings, and the lady continued to prophesy over her. She started reaching out to other people because her encounter with God was so real. She didn't tell anybody because she thought everyone would think she was weird.

Do we attend every service with expectancy? Do we wake up every morning knowing that God's presence is with us? Some people were raised in church all their life and have never experienced an encounter with God. Are we crying out for God's presence in every service we attend? Are we truly closing our eyes and lifting our hands, knowing that He can fill us full of Himself? That is the kind of faith that can initiate an encounter with Jesus, which is worth more than hundreds of counseling sessions.

Of course, you can experience God in your room alone, but there is a corporate anointing when we gather together as a body of believers. Where two or three are gathered together in His name, you can truly draw in and focus on the anointing. This corporate anointing creates an atmosphere for miracles to happen. When we are believing God for something, we enter the room and press in for it. Every service we attend, we say, "Lord, fill me. I want to feel your presence, and I want to know you are with me." Do you want to feel his presence? He designed us to feel his presence. Do you have close encounters with Him? Sometimes we get so dry that we do not even realize it. But when He comes in and fills you up, and your cup is overflowing, faith comes naturally; it is developed.

Faith will get you there. Anything else is boring and a waste of time. If something comes your way and does not align with complete abundance, healing, or whatever you need, look at it and say, "Get out of my way." We should be addicted to faith. We should crave faith. When Jesus is inside your heart, you cannot help it. You can only operate in faith when the King lives inside your heart. A child of God can only operate in faith.

If you study the book of Acts, you will read that the growth of the church was contingent on people encountering the Holy Ghost, and then they went out and shared what they had encountered. The reason why the church has declined in America is because they are not sharing Jesus, and the reason they are not sharing Jesus is because they do not know Him personally. People only share their faith when they have a relationship with Him. If you have something based on religion, it is dead. You can think you have a relationship, but all you have is religion. Then you will find yourself producing what religion produces, which is nothing. Growing pains hurt. Anything living is growing. So, if the church is not growing, it is not living. And Jesus is the true vine. When you have a revelation of Him, you are continually growing. If you find yourself stagnant, you need to figure out which god you are serving.

## Ever Increasing

He is the developer of our faith. Your faith should be ever-increasing because you are continually receiving from your source. Like I said in the first chapter if your job shuts down tomorrow and the banks close. You have no money; every cent is gone. All of your savings and investments are gone. We think it will never happen, but it has happened in the past. Remember World War I and World War II? What are you going to do? Is your source your job? Is your source your investment? Is your source your 401k? Is your source your rental properties? None of that can be your source; they can only be your tools. Christ has to be the source of everything in your life. If it all goes down the drain tomorrow, you must have faith in Jesus Christ; He will get you through whatever takes place.

God forbid that it will happen, but our faith should be at such a level that if it does, we will not run around like the rest of the world, acting like chickens with our heads cut off. We will be in our right mind, not our emotions, and say, "It doesn't matter. The world did not give me this joy, and the world cannot take it away. The peace that I have, the favor that I have, the world did not give it to me, the government did not give it to me, mama and daddy did not give it to me, it does not matter what happens, I have it, and I am going to keep it." That is why you cannot freak out over what is happening in this world. If you know your source, you will not panic. The Lord is the developer of our faith. If He brings us to it, He will bring us through it.

God begins to develop our faith when we put it on the line. How do you put your faith on the line? First, the Word of God must be preeminent in your life. It has to be your roadmap. It has to be your manual. People say, "I believe the Bible, but I just don't take it literally." Then you do not believe in the Bible. You have to believe every word. I understand there are different interpretations. I believe all translations from front to back and everything in between. The Word must be foremost, and you must base all your decisions on it. Jesus was the Word made flesh. When you put the Word first, you effectively give Jesus Christ preeminence in your life. Second, you have to meditate on the Word. You actually have to stop and think about what you are reading and then apply it to your life.

We have to realize that faith is not just about us. People are watching our faith. They might say no to Jesus today or tomorrow, but when they hit that bump in life and are at the end of their rope, they will be drawn to the men and women of faith. They have observed us going through our situations and have seen faith rise up in us. That will lead the people around us to salvation more than anything. The world is watching how we handle our situations. They are watching where our faith is. If we are panicking like everyone else, we don't have anything they don't have. I do not believe in stocking food for the next hundred years. What happens when the neighborhood finds out? They are coming to take our food, and there are not enough guns to stop them. The food will not save us, but our faith in God will. When you put the Word first and meditate on the Word, you are building the capacity for immense faith. It is time for the church to start believing for the money to take this gospel to the next level. We need to take our faith to the level that we own the banks that hold the money. We have to believe for control over everything that influences the narrative of Christ. We must take over our schools, banks, parliaments, government, etc. The only way to do this is with radical ever-increasing faith.

You have to act on the Word. It is not enough to put it first and just meditate on it. James 2:17 states, *So also faith by itself, if it does not have works, is dead.* Faith without works is dead. Faith begins to grow when the Word becomes a vital part of your daily conduct and speech. We have to speak the Word on a daily basis; we have to walk out that Word. It is not enough to read your devotional. You have to act on the Word of God. When faith begins to grow, the devil's dominion begins to wane, and circumstances begin to lose their force over our lives. The more your faith increases, the more the devil's dominion decreases. The more faith you have, the less fear you will have. The more faith you have, the more little things will quit messing up the bigger things. We have to take our faith to the next level. Then we have to act on the Word. You have to decide you are going to live by faith, not by Blue Cross or Blue Shield. You have the Old Rugged Cross and the Shield of Faith. The just shall live by faith. You have to live a life of love because, without love, faith does not work. You have to love God and love people.

## Black Belt Confidence

It is radical, but things can change in a moment. As quickly as you can flip a coin, God can change your situation at that moment. We took our son to his karate class, and I began laughing at him. My wife asked, "What are you laughing about?" I said, "Isaac is acting like a Black Belt." It was his second day. I thought, "Faith it until you make it," not *fake* it, *faith* it. Sometimes you show up at a scenario and think it is out of your league. However, it is not out of God's league. You have to show up with the confidence of a Black Belt. Before you obtain it in the natural, you already have it in the spiritual. We are already seated in heavenly places. You already have the victory when you show up with that Black Belt faith. Just have that mentality, "I am going to *faith* it until I make it." You don't have to look surprised or shocked, just know you have it.

I said that laughingly, but my son is convinced, with all confidence, that he is good in karate. He is convinced in his faith. Are you convinced in your faith? Are you fully persuaded that *He that has begun a good work in you is faithful to finish it* (Philippians 1:6)? Are you fully persuaded in your faith that God will protect you and your family against a virus? Even when the numbers are climbing, are you fully persuaded? Do you have confidence that he is going to keep you? He said He will keep you. Are you fully persuaded that he will heal you, restore your marriage, and give you the spouse for whom you are believing? Are you fully persuaded, with all boldness, that he is not a man that He should lie? He is going to take care of you because you are His child and the apple of His eye.

# CHAPTER 3

*Faith on Fire:*
## Turning Things Around

Is it possible to turn your situation around? Many people believe when they are struggling in life, they have just received the bad luck of the draw. Their circumstances are by happenstance, and they can do nothing about it.

Hebrews 11:1-3 declares:

Now faith is the substance of things hoped for, the evidence of things not seen. For by it the elders obtained a good testimony. By faith we understand that the worlds were framed by the word of God, so that the things which are seen were not made of things which are visible. (NKJV)

If the unseen force of faith ignited God's own Word to form the worlds and He made us in His own image, then our faith can turn around any situation we may ever face. Faith can turn the table on any attack of the devil. Faith can turn what the devil meant for evil into a blessing. Faith can turn anything around to your benefit if you will believe and trust wholeheartedly in God's goodness and mercy.

In the book of Genesis, we find the story of a man named Joseph who faced betrayal and unjust treatment and suffered one setback after another. Despite crippling circumstances, including a stint in prison, Joseph continued to trust in the love, goodness, and faithfulness of God. If God is a good God, which He is, and you are walking with Him and walking in His Word, you cannot lose. No matter what happens in your life, even if you don't understand what is going on, your faith will cause things to ultimately work out for your good. Faith in God's love and faithfulness to His Word creates an all-encompassing shield around you.

When you refuse to fear, the devil cannot do anything in your life. When your faith is in God, it is impossible for the devil to succeed against you. Every attack and negative circumstance must turn around for your good, as it did for Joseph. Joseph ended up exactly where God wanted him. He was made second in command over all of Egypt, and God used him to save the lives of many people (Genesis 50:20). God used all of the negative situations Joseph experienced to prepare and train him for success in his assignment in life. Praise God that every challenge you face is nothing more than an opportunity to exercise your faith in His Word, gain greater wisdom, and become better equipped to handle the calling that is on your life. Never crumple in the face of adverse situations. Your plans may not have worked out the way you expected, but God has everything in control. Faith in God and His Word can turn anything around for your good.

## No Fear

1 John 4:18 states, *There is no fear in love; but perfect love casts out fear, because fear involves torment. But he who fears has not been made perfect in love* (NKJV). Fear is the devil's doorway into the life of a believer. When you allow fear to enter your life, spiritual forces that open you up to the works of the enemy are released. Fear is simply faith that has been perverted. Fear is actually faith in the devil's ability to harm you. You should never allow fear to have any place in your thoughts. The Word of God through love is the way to combat fear because we know that perfect love casts out fear. God loves you, and

28

His plans for you are good. It is never God's plan that you suffer from any kind of torment brought on by fear.

The root of fear is doubt that God really loves you. But when you take the time to meditate on God's perfect, pure, and unconditional love for you, that love will cast out the fear. Once you have a revelation of the depth of your Father God's love for you, you will fear nothing. The Word of God says in 2 Timothy 1:7, *For God has not given us a spirit of fear, but of power and of love and of a sound mind.* What is there to fear when God is on your side? Meditate on the cross. Think about the love that God has for you. Receive that love. Soak in that love. When you know and believe in God's love towards you, fear has to leave. So clothe yourself in the love of God and fight fear with everything you have. Have no fear!

## A Spiritual Force

Faith is not a mental exercise but a spiritual force. If you live by faith, you will develop the right mental attitude and begin to think positively based on God's Word. When you are facing pressure, you should get ready to do something that may be difficult. It may demand discipline. A real "Word" person is strong, determined, and resolute! When you become strong in the Word of God, you will say, like the song, "I shall not be moved. I'm just like a tree planted by the river." That is the voice of a strong-willed person who knows where they stand in God's Word. They are determined that if anybody moves, it will just have to be the devil. This kind of attitude does not come to you overnight. You must feed on God's Word day and night until you know that you know that you know. Many people are inspired by the message of faith. It sounds good to them, and they run out and say, "Bless God, I am going to do this! I will not be moved!" Let me warn you: don't try to live on something that is not a revelation to *you* personally.

But, when the Word is deeply rooted in your heart, stand your ground until the devil backs off. When you base your confession on the authority of God's Word, and you are deeply rooted in it, then you can say with confidence, "I will not be moved by my circumstance," and it will come with joy and assurance. You will know that nothing the devil brings your way will cause you to be shaken! You have become strong-willed in the Word of God.

## More than Conquerors

Romans 8:37 says, *Yet in all these things we are more than conquerors through Him who loved us* (NKJV). A conqueror is one who has entered the ring, who has fought and won and has gained the title or trophy. Someone who is described as "more than a conqueror" is one who has been handed the title and trophy without doing a thing. Jesus is the one who fought the enemy and won, but He gave the title and trophy to you. He has already made you more than a conqueror; you just need to believe it and receive it personally. You may say, "But, Pastor Brandon, how can I be more than a conqueror when I feel like such a loser?" The answer is simple: make the decision to no longer see yourself as a loser. Once you have made this decision, stop saying things such as, "This won't work for me; I can't win because of where I came from; I can't win because of what happened to me in the past." When you are in Christ, none of these things make a difference. If you have made Jesus your Lord, the Bible declares that you are more than a conqueror! When you have this revelation in your heart, you will think, walk, and talk like the winner you are. Defeat will be a thing of the past, all bondage will be broken, and failure will never again be an option because you are more than a conqueror.

## God is on Your Side

Romans 8:31-32 declares, *...If God is for us, who can be against us? He who did not spare His own Son, but delivered Him up for us all, how shall He not with Him also freely give us all things* (NKJV)? There are a lot of Christians who are not convinced that God is for them. They mistakenly think God is somehow partly to blame for the bad things that happen to them (never mind their poor choices and decisions). How would you like to be commander-in-chief of an army where half of your troops do not even know who the enemy is? They have their weapons pointed toward headquarters, blaming you for all of their problems. As ridiculous as that sounds, it is not an inadequate description of God's army.

It is common for people to tell me about a particular trial they are facing and then ask, "Why did God let this happen to me?" They do not realize that God is not against them; he is for them! Jesus made it clear who our enemy is when He said in 1 Peter 5:8, *Your adversary the devil walks about like a roaring lion, seeking whom he may devour* (NKJV). John 10:10 says, *The thief does not come except to steal, and to kill, and to destroy* (NKJV). He went on in the same verse to say, *I have come that they may have life, and that they may have it more abundantly.* It is the devil who comes to steal from you and try to destroy you. God is a good God; everything He does is for your good and for your benefit. He will never ever cause a harmful situation in your life to prove something to you or to teach you something. You are so loved by God that He is willing to give you freely all things to enjoy. God is on your side!

## Not Us, Him

Philippians 3:9-10 declares:

And be found in him, not having mine own righteousness, which is of the law, but that which is through faith of Christ, the righteousness which is of God by faith: That I may know Him, and the power of His resurrection, (NKJV)

When you believe who the Word says you are, you will expect every adversity to turn into a victory. You begin to expect success only when you see yourself as God sees you. As long as you are looking at your own merits, you will have an element of self-doubt. You will question whether God is going to show you favor in life. What you have done and who you are has nothing to do with favor and success. That is good news because, without Jesus, we are nothing! God's favor and God's honor cannot be earned. You did not earn His favor, and you did not earn His honor; Jesus earned it for you! Even though Jesus earned it for you, it is still your responsibility to walk in it by faith and let God's favor become a reality in your life. God sees you as righteous, above reproach, and worthy to be blessed with success. He delights to crown you with glory and honor. Why would He not give you abundant favor and success in your life? Believe who the Word says you are. See yourself as He sees you. Then you will expect every adversity to turn into a victory. You will expect success today.

## Press Forward

Romans 4:20-21 says, *He did not waver at the promise of God through unbelief, but was strengthened in faith, giving glory to God, and being fully convinced that what He had promised He was also able to perform* (NKJV). The Scripture verse above speaks of Abraham, who, after many years, had not yet received what God had promised to him. Despite the lack of manifestation, he still believed God's goodness was ahead of him. Perhaps you are waiting to see God's promised goodness in your life. I can tell you that what God has for you is not behind you or off to the side, waiting for you to chase it down; it is ahead of you. The Israelites were deceived into thinking their goodness was behind them in Egypt. They delayed receiving God's promise because they kept looking behind instead of pressing forward on the path of obedience and trust. Then when they were tired of waiting for Moses to return from the mountain, they attempted to create their own good thing by forging a golden idol and having a party. As a result of their disobedience, many people lost their lives. Do not be deceived. God is a good God. You do not need to make good things happen in your own strength. God's goodness is not behind you; it is ahead of you. The Bible says in James 1:16-17, *Do not be deceived, my beloved brethren. Every good gift and every perfect gift is from above, and comes down from the Father of lights* (NKJV). Do not waiver at the promise of God through unbelief, but be strengthened in faith. Believe and trust in the goodness of God that is ahead, and then press forward into all He has for you.

# CHAPTER 4

## Faith on Fire:
## Six Greatest Hindrances of Faith

What are some of the things that obstruct us from walking in faith? We will cover six of the greatest hindrances to our faith.

Jesus explains in Mark 11:22-24 how to have faith in God:

And Jesus answering saith unto them, Have faith in God. For verily I say unto you, That whosoever shall say unto this mountain, Be thou removed, and be thou cast into the sea; and shall not doubt in his heart, but shall believe that those things which he saith shall come to pass; he shall have whatsoever he saith. Therefore I say unto you, What things soever ye desire, when ye pray, believe that ye receive them, and ye shall have them. (KJV)

When you pray, when do you believe your prayer is coming to pass? Answer: the very moment you pray because Hebrews 11:1 states, *Now faith is the substance of things hoped for and the evidence of things not seen.* You have to believe that when you are praying, you should give thanks to God for performing whatever you are asking for. When you speak it out of your mouth, He will do it in that very moment. How should you respond after you pray? You should just thank God that your prayers are answered and that the victory has already been given to you. What is faith? *Now faith is the substance of things hoped for...* Remember, faith and confidence are the same. So if you have faith, you have confidence. Are you confident in some area of your life? Then you have faith in your ability to conduct yourself or do your job in that area. So when you have faith in God, you have confidence in His Word that He is not a man that He should lie. If He said it, He will do it. He will do it and bring it to pass in your life.

## The New Creation

The first hindrance to our faith is a lack of understanding of the new creation. 2 Corinthians 5:17 says, *Therefore if any man be in Christ, he is a new creature: old things are passed away; behold, all things are become new.* Old things are passed away is in the past tense. Behold all things become new is in the present tense. Colossians 1:22 says, *In the body of his flesh through death, to present you holy and unblameable and unreproveable in his sight.* 1 Peter 1:23 says, *Being born again, not of corruptible seed, but of incorruptible, by the word of God, which liveth and abideth for ever.*

Revelation 1:5-6 declares,

And from Jesus Christ, who is the faithful witness, and the first begotten of the dead, and the prince of the kings of the earth. Unto him that loved us, and washed us from our sins in his own blood, And hath made us kings and priests unto God and his Father; to him be glory and dominion forever and ever. Amen. (KJV)

Again, 2 Corinthians 5:17 says, *Therefore if any man be in Christ, he is a new creature and the old things pass away.* The enemy works through the carnality of our mind. The carnality of our mind always wants to remind us of our past negative actions. I have witnessed this many times, counseling people throughout the years. Many parents raise their children a certain way because they feel bad for what they have experienced in life, so they try to make up for it through their kids. When the truth is, God has already forgiven them. Their sin has already been washed away because they have been made new.

It is not the enemy, but your mind, will, intellect, and emotions are reminding you of your past. The Word of God says that your sin is as far as the East is from the West. If you are going to walk in faith, you cannot walk in faith and condemnation simultaneously. If you look at the story in the Bible of the man born blind, they asked who sinned. Did the father sin? Did the mother sin? Did he sin? Jesus said that nobody sinned. This was designed so that the glory of God could be revealed. You never see Jesus approaching a sinner and saying, "Look what you did; that was so horrible; you must be punished." But you do see Jesus dealing harshly with religious people. If you are walking in genuine faith, you are not walking in condemnation.

The enemy will attempt to tie you down to something you did twenty years ago to keep you from moving forward in God's calling for your life. But, the minute you say Jesus come into my heart, be my Lord and Savior, you receive the calling over the comfort. You will stand out immediately. Did Jesus have a calling? When He comes and lives inside our hearts, we have a calling over our comfort. And so the enemy will next attack us with an attempt to stop that calling because that is his assignment, right? The devil will say, "Oh, I don't want her doing that. I don't want her preaching the gospel. I don't want him speaking the Word of God. I will put some condemnation on them to stop their calling." That is the assignment of the enemy. The enemy's assignment is to stop your calling.

When we get revelation of what God says, we will begin to focus on what we are called to do. If the enemy slaps condemnation on us over and over, we just keep reminding him and ourselves by quoting, *There is therefore now no condemnation for those who are in Christ Jesus.* He might remind us a hundred times throughout the day, but our calling will always set us apart. The minute you are born again and become a new creation, you receive the calling over the comfort.

Let's review the born-again experience. When we use the word *apostolic*, we refer to a New Testament church. We are not in the Old Testament or under the old covenant. We all should be very happy about that. I can promise that if we were under the old covenant, having to obey the Ten Commandments with hundreds of laws attached, we could not go a day without breaking at least one of them. So we should just thank God that we are not an Old Testament church; we are a New Testament church concerning salvation and a born-again experience. In everything you do, God has lined out the path in your life; He already knew what you would do before you did it. As a matter of fact, Romans 8:8 expounds, *And we know that all things work together for good to them that love God, to them who are the called according to his purpose.*

Many churches are uncomfortable talking about the subject of predestination. Romans 8:29 affirms we are predestined by stating, *For whom he did foreknow, he also did predestinate to be conformed to the image of his Son, that he might be the firstborn among many brethren.* John 15:16 explains it this way, *You did not choose me, but I chose you and appointed you so that you might go and bear fruit - fruit that will last - and so that whatever you ask in my name the Father will give you* (NIV). God chooses you. What about free will? Here is an example. What will you decide if I point a gun to your head and tell you to choose life or death? You would choose life, right? Therefore, you made the choice, but God still got what He wanted in your life. God allows you to be put in situations where you choose His will over your own will because He is more interested in getting you to fulfill your purpose and destiny than you are.

The New Testament church believes Romans 10:9-10 as part of the born-again process (see John 3:3-6).

Paul said:

That if thou shalt confess with thy mouth the Lord Jesus, and shalt believe in thine heart that God hath raised him from the dead, thou shalt be saved. For with the heart man believeth unto righteousness; and with the mouth confession is made unto salvation. (KJV)

I believe the first part of salvation is confessing Jesus, to identify Christ as our savior. But it does not stop there; that plants the seed. The next step is water baptism (see Acts 2:37-39), which represents the old man being buried with Christ in the ground, and then the new man is resurrected with Christ. The old is washed away, and the new creation begins. This is called sanctification. We cannot earn salvation. Sanctification is the process that converts your mind because when you confess Christ and are baptized, your spirit is saved. Remember, I am a spirit, I have a soul (will, emotions, and mind), and I live in a body. I am not three separate individuals; I am the same person. Now when you confess Jesus, and you are baptized, your spirit is saved. The conversion of the mind causes your behavior to line up with what your spirit has already received.

## Our Place in Him and His Place in Us

The second hindrance to our faith is the lack of understanding of our place in Him and His in us. In Christ, in Him, and in Whom, occurs one hundred and thirty-four times in the New Testament. This avows who we are and what we have. Colossians 3:11 says, *Where there is neither Greek nor Jew, circumcision nor uncircumcision, Barbarian, Scythian, bond nor free: but Christ is all, and in all.* Ephesians 3:6 affirms, *That the Gentiles should be fellow heirs, and of the same body, and partakers of his promise in Christ by the gospel;*

39

We are in Christ. If we do not understand that we are in Him and He is in us, we never function in the full capacity of our faith; we will always doubt who we are. But there is a difference between Christ in You and You in Christ. Christ within us is the hope of glory. Many people never get this revelation because Christ is with them, but they are not with Christ. Colossians 1:27 states, *To whom God would make known what is the riches of the glory of this mystery among the Gentiles; which is Christ in you, the hope of glory:* Christ is in you, the hope of glory. He cannot be in you when you are not living the new creation or when you are not living in righteousness. You are not in right standing with God because you never got in Him. You never surrendered to Him.

If we look at Jesus, He was ridiculed; He was persecuted; and He suffered. The minute anything becomes difficult, we start questioning, "Oh God, what is going on," but we read 1 Peter 2:9, which states, *But ye are a chosen generation, a royal priesthood, an holy nation, a peculiar people; that ye should shew forth the praises of him who hath called you out of darkness into his marvelous light.* All these things stand out: a chosen generation, a royal priesthood, a holy nation, and a peculiar people. When you think about priesthood, you think of kings and queens. When we are His own special people, we will stand out. We are going to look a little different; if we do not look different or peculiar, we need to do a temperature check on ourselves.

I think of the life of Noah. It is so fascinating that he built an ark 510 feet long. Can you imagine that? I mean, God asks us to do something a little crazy, and we say, "Oh gosh, what are my neighbors going to think?" What is this or that person going to think? What does God think? That is the most critical question to ask. But Noah built it 510 feet long; that is long; everybody could see it. Envision everyone thinking you were that crazy. Then literal destruction comes and wipes everyone away, but guess who was still living? The greater the persecution is, the greater the glory.

Look at Jesus. The Word declares that He is seated at the right hand of the Father, and every knee shall bow, and every tongue shall confess His name. Yet, He hung on the cross, and people mocked Him. When you are experiencing something that is really hard, when you are walking in faith, and everyone is pointing their finger at you, and you stand out like a sore thumb, this is your chance to shine. Or when you are on your job, and everybody thinks you are a nut because you will not go along with what everyone else is doing; remember, this is your chance to shine. When you are quiet, God shows up as your vindicator. You do not have to say anything because your enemies are silenced; that is called the walk of faith. That is the test of faith. It was a test of faith for Noah to build something extraordinary. When Christ is in you, they are not persecuting you; they are persecuting Him.

## Righteousness

The third hindrance to our faith is the lack of understanding of righteousness. This holds more people in bondage than anything else because people do not understand righteousness and what it gives. James 5:16 says, *Confess your faults one to another, and pray one for another, that ye may be healed. The effectual fervent prayer of a righteous man availeth much.* In order for our prayers to be answered, it has to come out of righteousness. Answered prayer flows out of righteousness. According to the New Testament, good works do not produce righteousness. Righteousness produces good works. Many people try to get righteous by how they dress; I am not saying that you should go and dress like you are going to the club. We do not judge people who dress that way even though we don't because we are set apart, right? People will perform works to present themselves as more righteous, but the only person they are deceiving is themselves because only Christ makes you righteous. When He saves you, you become righteous. Righteousness is imparted to you. You receive righteousness; you do not work for it. Self-righteousness will relegate you into bondage.

You have people who are self-righteous; on the flip side, you have people who think they can never be righteous. They use the terminology, "I'm just a sinner saved by grace." That is not what that Scripture says. It says you *were* a sinner, but *now* you are saved by grace. Somebody said, "How do I receive righteousness? You receive righteousness by believing that through Christ, He has made you righteous. It comes back to your faith. You have to believe. You must believe it in your heart and allow what is in your heart to affect your thinking and emotions. Then it has to go from your thinking and emotions to your behavior and actions.

To be honest, I get a little concerned when people just hone in on sin all the time. All they talk about is sin, sin, and sin, or all they preach about is sin, sin, and more sin. In my profession, I discovered that most of the time, self-righteousness is usually a smoke screen to hide what is really going on behind closed doors. Did you catch that? If you believe you are unrighteous, you will always act unrighteous. You are going to do unrighteous things. You are going to lie; you are going to steal; you are going to do all those things labeled sin. But if you believe you are righteous through Jesus Christ and receive that righteousness, you will begin to believe you are righteous and produce righteous works; you are not performing works to receive righteousness.

There are a lot of fancy slogans people coin as bible verses, such as, "God only helps those who help themselves." Obviously, there are Scriptures that say, "Faith without works is dead," etc. However, people recite non-scriptural *churchisms* geared toward earning righteousness. Observe your thoughts, motives, and actions and ask, "Am I doing this to try and get somewhere, or do I believe I am already there?" Burnout comes from trying to achieve righteousness. You already know it cannot be achieved, so you will get tired and weary trying to get somewhere you already are. I always use the example that you are trying to sit in a chair that you are already sitting in. You're there; you're already there! And then you become frustrated as a believer because you are trying to sit down in something you are already sitting in. You spend your life trying to achieve something and end up on your deathbed, wondering if you accomplished it. That is a distraction the enemy uses to deter you from moving forward because you are too busy spinning your wheels trying to accomplish something you already have.

When we try to earn our righteousness, we have not truly received Him for the remission of our sins. We do not have a revelation of what was accomplished at Calvary. We do not have a revelation of the crucifixion and resurrection. Every time you try to do it yourself, you are asking Jesus to get back on the cross because the first time was not good enough for you. You have to receive the revelation that you are the righteousness of God in Him. 2 Corinthians 5:21 proclaims, *For he hath made him to be sin for us, who knew no sin; that we might be made the righteousness of God in him.* How do you receive it? We receive it by faith. Everything flows through the channel of faith.

## The Name

The fourth hindrance to our faith is the lack of understanding of our privilege and right to use the name of Jesus. The name of Christ is the key, or the seal, or the ticket to everything in the apostolic or New Testament church. Acts 4:7 says, "They asked, By what power, or by what name, have ye done this?" Throughout the New Testament, they repeatedly asked, "By what name?" Whose name? They asked Jesus, "By what name do you cast out these devils."

Mark 16:17-18 says:

And these signs shall follow them that believe; In my name shall they cast out devils; they shall speak with new tongues; They shall take up serpents; and if they drink any deadly thing, it shall not hurt them; they shall lay hands on the sick, and they shall recover. (KJV)

We understand this does not mean picking up a snake or chugging some Drano to test your faith. But we do have an assurance that if we have faith in His Word and a snake bites us, it will not harm us, or if somebody poisons us, God will protect us. He is going to watch over us. If God's Word is on the inside of you, He said that He watches over his Word to perform it. If the Word has been sown into your life, He is going to make sure the Word performs in your life.

John 14:12-13 declares:

Verily, verily, I say unto you, He that believeth on me, the works that I do shall he do also; and greater works than these shall he do; because I go unto my Father. And whatsoever ye shall ask in my name, that will I do... (KJV)

We must have faith and understand that we have been given the name. The name is the stamp of approval on everything we ask and believe God for. We pray in the name of Jesus. We exercise our authority in the name of Jesus. Everything we do is by the name of Jesus Christ in the New Testament church. John 16:23 says, *And in that day ye shall ask me nothing. Verily, verily, I say unto you, Whatsoever ye shall ask the Father in my name, he will give it you.* When Jesus communicates this Scripture, He is not speaking regarding a third person. He is speaking in a parable to communicate with the religious people in that moment. He is not talking about someone because he said, "If you have seen me, you have seen the father." He is teaching them based on what they came out of and communicating something that no one on earth has ever heard.

## Just Do It

The fifth hindrance to our faith is the lack of understanding regarding acting on the Word. Proverbs 3:5 states, *Trust in the LORD with all thine heart; and lean not unto thine own understanding.* We have to rely totally on the Word. Your mind will always attempt to make logical sense out of everything. Jesus walking on water does not make logical sense. Healing lepers does not make logical sense. There are many things God will ask us to do that will never make logical sense in our minds. It will require our faith. It will require our obedience. The flesh always wants to arrange things where we do not need faith. We will try to rationalize it in our minds and map it all out, but in the end, we still need a miracle. And even if we do figure it out, God will ask us to do something else that requires another miracle on another level. We will always need faith.

When you do something that requires serious faith, you must know that God has called you to do it. Every day as believers, God is calling us to trust in Him. No matter how we try to arrange it, He will always pull the rug out from under us so that we have to depend on Him. He is just that jealous of us. Hebrews 11:6 states, *But without faith it is impossible to please...* That tells us that we have to walk in faith to please him. So obviously, He is calling us to stretch faith beyond our ability. Concerning any situation, the only question necessary is, "But what does God say?" What does He say in His word? Faith is about acting on the Word. It is not good enough to hear it and believe it. You have to act on it. Do not be deceived; believing demands action. James 1:22 says, *But be ye doers of the word, and not hearers only, deceiving your own selves.*

If you only hear the Word of God without acting on it, you are only performing a religion. Nothing is produced from it. I hate to break the news to you. You actually have to believe the Word of God literally, and you have to practice it literally. John 3:21 says, *But he that doeth truth cometh to the light, that his deeds may be made manifest, that they are wrought in God.* The truth represents the Word of God. So he that acts on the Word comes to the light, and God will produce his deeds. In other words, anytime you are a doer and act on the Word, He will bring you to victory. He is going to bring you through it. Luke 8:21 says, *And he answered and said unto them, My mother and my brethren are these which hear the word of God, and do it.* As the Nike slogan says, "Just do it."

## Speak Right

The sixth hindrance of our faith is the lack of understanding on holding fast to the confession of our faith. Hebrews 4:14 says, *Seeing then that we have a great high priest, that is passed into the heavens, Jesus the Son of God, let us hold fast our profession [confession].*

Our faith keeps pace with our confession. The more you speak it out of your mouth, the more your faith will increase. I am not moved by what I see but by what I believe. We are moved by what we believe. What do we believe? We believe the Word of God, the Bible. Fear to act or confess before you have the manifestation is to doubt God's Word in your life. I have heard this a million times, and God bless them. I know they are sincere. They make the statement, "Pastor, when God blesses me with a lot of money, I am going to give the church a big chunk of it." I want to respond, "Don't worry about it; He is not going to bless you because you are waiting for him to give you something first. God does not work for tips." A man can never reap a harvest unless his seed is in the ground first. They have it backward. There will never be a harvest if a seed is never planted. The seed produces the harvest. You must be willing to act on God's Word and believe that if you sow a seed, He will give you the harvest.

Every day, we have an opportunity to speak the opposite of what we see. For example, if you have a child acting out, instead of saying, "You need to act right," you could say, "In the name of Jesus, you are a well-behaved kid." Instead of complaining about their spouses, one should start speaking positively about their life by calling them into more extraordinary things. We should confess that we have spheres of influence; we have land; we have property; and we have an unlimited supply of resources. We have to believe it. It can be scary to dream and think like that. The enemy wants us to limit ourselves when we speak. He wants us to curse ourselves instead of speaking our blessings into existence.

We live within a world system where everyone is eager to diagnose people with a label. Most people do not understand that the people who make diagnoses have shares and stocks in what they prescribe. So for the money, they diagnose everyone and slap a title on them. To me, that is horrible. It is like putting a curse on them. Now you can see how important it is to speak the right things. We must put the Word of God, which is the truth, in a more prominent place in our lives. We must hold fast to the confession of our faith. Here are some confessions based on the Word of God.

Speak them out loud:

1. I declare the absolute lordship of Jesus. He is Lord of all things in my life. He is lordship over everything. There is nothing above Him. He is over every president and every king. He is over all the nations of the world.

2. I declare Psalm 23:1: *The LORD is my shepherd; I shall not want.* I shall not want. I will live a life of never wanting because He gives me the desires of my heart. If He takes care of the birds of the air, how much more will my heavenly father take care of me? I do not have to want.

3. I declare Peter 5:7: *Casting all your care upon him; for he careth for you.* I do not have a care. Why? Because I cast it on Jesus, and He cares for me.

4. I declare Isaiah 53:3-5:

He is despised and rejected of men; a man of sorrows, and acquainted with grief: and we hid as it were our faces from him; he was despised, and we esteemed him not. Surely he hath borne our griefs, and carried our sorrows: yet we did esteem him stricken, smitten of God, and afflicted. But he was wounded for our transgressions, he was bruised for our iniquities: the chastisement of our peace was upon him; and with his stripes we are healed. (KJV)

I believe that every sickness, disease, sorrow, and grief was laid on Jesus at the cross. I am free from all diseases. I am free. I am free because His word says I am.

5. I declare 1 Corinthians 1:30: *But of him are ye in Christ Jesus, who of God is made unto us wisdom, and righteousness, and sanctification, and redemption:* Jesus is made unto me wisdom, righteousness, sanctification, and redemption. I am wise, righteous, sanctified, and redeemed. Praise the Lord!

Many good and faithful Christians miss out on enjoying the truth of the blessings of God because their confession binds them. Do not be bound by your confession. Stay calm and speak the right things. As humans, we tend to want to fill up space with words. You then find yourself feeling empty, speaking thoughts that have no meaning in conversation because you merely desire conversation. And then you realize it was not fruitful. It was not full of faith. But you felt obligated to say something. Sometimes, it is okay to be quiet. It is better to be silent than to speak negatively and have to walk back your words. Do not say anything if you feel a negative thought rising in your mind. If you can't speak faith, then don't speak? Spiritual maturity means realizing when things do not require your response. It is like the person sitting behind you at a traffic light. They are honking, wanting you to go, and you are thinking, "I'm at a red light. If I go, I might get killed." They are impatient, wanting you to go, and you almost want to go because the person is honking at you, but it would actually endanger your life. There are times when people will put pressure on you to say or do something. Do not let them pressure you into it; it could endanger your life!

I will never forget a story my father-in-law shared with me. He was in the Army Special Forces, and his unit carried out missions that evacuated people from bad areas and situations. On this occasion, they were under fire and surrounded by the enemy. My father-in-law just sat there, got a book out, opened it, and started reading while bullets were flying. The individual they were protecting on this mission asked, "How can you just stop and read a book? How can you do that? My father-in-law calmly responded, "Just settle down; we are going to make it out of here safely." He was confessing it. Let me tell you, he had to confess and speak over his circumstances to be alive today after having been in such volatile situations for over twenty years. He would confess, "We are going to survive this. We are going to make it out." That is what we have to do to survive our circumstances. We must get our confession in line with God's blessing. Speak the Word of God over your situations. Amen!

# CHAPTER 5

## Faith on Fire:
## Have Faith in God

The Lord said this to me so clearly: "Your faith-begging days are over." I want you to receive this in your spirit. Your faith will no longer beg for what you desire.

Matthew 11:12-14 declare:

And on the morrow, when they were come from Bethany, he was hungry: And seeing a fig tree afar off having leaves, he came, if haply he might find any thing thereon: and when he came to it, he found nothing but leaves; for the time of figs was not yet. And Jesus answered and said unto it, No man eat fruit of thee hereafter for ever. And his disciples heard it. (KJV)

Now what you have to understand about the fig tree is that from a distance, the fig tree projects or looks like it has fruit. But all it has are leaves. It presents itself as fruit but doesn't really possess any fruit. And when I read this Scripture, God said to me, "Your faith is not going to just produce leaves any longer." I am going to show you how to go from bearing leaves to bearing fruit in your faith. Our faith produces.

The Bible says that every man has been given a measure of faith. But we have to ask ourselves, "What is our faith producing?" Are we producing leaves, or are we producing fruit? Now what is faith? Hebrews 11:1 explains, *Now faith is the substance of things hoped for and the evidence of things not seen.* Faith is laying hold of the unrealities and bringing them into reality by acting on the Word of God. What is the opposite of faith? The opposite of faith is fear. What is fear? Fear is the substance of things not hoped for and the evidence of things that are seen by the natural eye. So fear is always the opposite of faith.

## Third Dimension of Faith

Now every man has been given a measure of faith, but God is always calling us into an ever-increasing faith. Our faith should not stay at one level. For instance, when you study the Tabernacle, it has three dimensions: the outer court, the inner court, and the holy of holies, the most holy place. Luke 2:11 says, *For unto you is born this day in the city of David a Saviour, which is Christ the Lord.* Notice that the Word states a Savior, Christ (Christos), and then the Lord. In your progression or walk with God, first, He is your Savior; second, He becomes Christ; and third, He becomes your Lord. The order is Savior, Christ, the Lord. You have to go from the outer court to the inner court to the most holy place. He becomes Lord to you in the most holy place.

When you get saved and accept Christ, He is your Savior. When you begin to get the revelation of the finished work of the cross, He becomes Christ to you. But then, you step into the third dimension behind the veil where God is calling all of us. The problem is that we get stuck in the outer court. We get stuck at Savior. Or we get stuck in Christ and never experience Him as Lord in our lives. So your faith has the same increase. Your faith should ever be increasing. We must understand that the Lord is not just calling us to stay in the outer or inner court. He is saying, "I want to take you beyond the veil, behind the veil, and show you who I really am and what I can do in your life, but I cannot do it unless you are willing to move in that direction with your faith." We have to grow our faith from producing leaves to producing fruit. You ask, "How do I do that?" I am glad you asked.

I am about to show you something that is unbelievable; you are going to be shocked. Mark 11:22 says, *And Jesus answering saith unto them, Have faith in God.* How do I go from leaves to fruit? Have faith in God; not faith in my job, not in my family, not in my government, not in anything else. I don't have faith in anything but God. He tells them to have faith in God. I am about to trip you up. He did not say to have faith in the Word. He said have faith in God. John 5:39-40 says, *You search the Scriptures because you think they give you eternal life. But the Scriptures point to me! Yet you refuse to come to me to receive this life* (NLT). You will look for Him in the Scriptures but not find Him there because the only thing Scriptures do is point to Him. We establish our faith in God; we do not establish our faith in what we read. Everything has to point to Jesus in your life. He is your Savior, Christ, and Lord. The Bible points us to Christ, and we put our faith in Him, totally relying on Him one hundred percent in every area of our life.

Your faith owns what God owns. You are a faith owner, and your faith owns what God owns. Ephesians 3:20 *states, Now unto him that is able to do exceeding abundantly above all that we ask or think, according to the power that worketh in us.* Whose power is within us? Whose power is living on the inside of us? If we had a born-again experience, God is not somewhere high up on a throne. Your heart has become his throne. If He is living on the inside of you and his power is in you, that means that everything that He has belongs to you.

I will make it simple. Christ is Savior, Christ is Lord, but He is King of all kings, and you are a child of the King. So if he is king and ruler of all things and you are a child of the king, whatever belongs to Him is your divine inheritance. Genesis 1:26 says, *And God said, Let*

53

*us make man in our image, after our likeness: and let them have dominion over the fish of the sea, and over the fowl of the air, and over the cattle, and over all the earth, and over every creeping thing that creepeth upon the earth.* If you understand dominion, it means that God gave man the title deed over the earth. Now what is faith? Hebrews 11:1 says, "Faith is the assurance or the title deed of things hoped for..." (AMP). Your faith is the title deed to whatever you are believing God for.

Our faith has to go from producing leaves to producing fruit. You have to understand that you cannot go up and talk down. Your confession runs with the pace of your faith. What you are speaking determines where you are. You will mask your faith with your words if you are not careful. What about the life of Job? If you study the life of Job, you will find a lot of what he experienced was in correlation with the words that were coming out of his mouth. It was not that God was giving the devil full reign to take him out; it was what he was speaking out of his mouth. If you connect the words that he spoke with what happened in his life, you will find that he received exactly what he was speaking. He was being hung by his own tongue. Somebody said, "I'm just not that spiritual." I recommend that you examine your life and then review the words you are speaking. I can guarantee you that what you are speaking is what you are receiving. It is a spiritual law that is greater than a physical law.

If I want to go up, I need to talk up. I have to change the way I talk. I have to let faith rise in my heart. Jesus said in Matthew 12:34, *...for out of the abundance of the heart, the mouth speaketh.* Proverbs 23:7 states, *For as he thinketh in his heart, so is he...* Your heart is your belief system. So what you believe in your heart will come out of your mouth. Your heart affects your thinking, emotions, behavior, and actions. It goes from your heart to your *saku*, where we get the word *psyche,* where the word *soul* derives from, which refers to your mind, will, intellect, and emotions. So what you believe goes from your heart to your brain, comes out of your mouth, and then you begin to act on it. If you believe you are a sinner, you will think like a sinner, talk like a sinner, and act like a sinner. Your behavior will produce sin in your life. But if you believe you are the righteousness in Christ Jesus. If you believe you have received a measure of faith. If you believe that your faith owns what God owns, it will rise up out of your heart. It will get into your soul and convert your mind. It will work out of your mouth and into the atmosphere.

Mark 11:23 says:

For verily I say unto you, That whosoever shall say unto this mountain, Be thou removed, and be thou cast into the sea; and shall not doubt in his heart, but shall believe that those things which he saith shall come to pass; he shall have whatsoever he saith. (KJV)

You cannot operate in doubt and faith; doubt is the twin sister of fear. Fear and doubt cannot coexist with faith. It is either one or the other. You must choose this day whom you will serve, faith or fear, the Lord or something else. So it is not good merely to have it in your heart; you must be convinced and fully persuaded. You have to be fully persuaded that your faith works. Fully persuaded means nothing can talk me out of what God said in His Word.

Mark 11:24-25 says:

Therefore I say unto you, What things soever ye desire, when ye pray, believe that ye receive them, and ye shall have them. And when ye stand praying, forgive, if ye have ought against any: that your Father also which is in heaven may forgive you your trespasses. (KJV)

55

And when ye stand praying, forgive. So what stops me from producing fruit and only producing leaves? The answer is unforgiveness. Mark 11:26 continues, *But if ye do not forgive, neither will your Father which is in heaven forgive your trespasses.* The Bible says that only those who will see the kingdom are those with a clean hand and a pure heart (Psalm 24:3). What it really boils down to is what is in the heart. Your heart can have blockages which will cause you to need open heart surgery. We have unforgiveness in our hearts that is blocking our faith from moving out into the atmosphere. As faith-filled believers, we must walk in a constant state of forgiveness. We have to forgive seventy times seven. We have to walk in complete forgiveness. "But they lied on me," forgive them. "They stole from me," forgive them. "They did me wrong; you don't know what they did to me when I was a child," forgive them. Unforgiveness is not hurting them; it is hurting you. Forgive, forgive, and forgive.

## My Testimony of Forgiveness

When I was a little boy, we were in a Pentecostal church that was strict with a lot of legalism, but of course, there was a lot of good there, also. I thank God for my heritage and from where I came. My mom was a single mom until I was about six years old. This man started coming around my mom and coming to church and all those wonderful things. Some of you ladies know what I'm talking about. He started saying all the right things, tithing, giving, and shaking a little in the spirit. Next thing you know, my mom ends up dating him. Then she married him. When she married him, it was as if the light switch went from on to off. Suddenly, he went from a great guy to a devil from hell. There is no other way to put it. I am not exaggerating. He started having several extra-marital affairs. He was very abusive to my mother and I. The mental abuse was day in and day out.

My mom was being manipulated. They would split up, and he would whine, cry, and apologize to get her back. They finally separated and divorced. If someone is abusing you, you have biblical reasons to divorce them. Nobody should stay in an abusive relationship, be it physical or emotional. He was very cruel to my brother also, which led him down the path of drug addiction and prison. When people battle drug addiction, it is a miracle if they survive it. In my teenage years, I struggled with all the hatred I developed because of what this man put my family through.

As a teenager, I was starting to get into ministry and travel. During my study time, the Lord would press on my heart to forgive him, and I would hear the Lord say in my spirit, "Forgive." And I would say, "But Lord, he deserves to be in prison." The Lord would say, "Forgive." "But Lord." "Forgive." And He just kept saying, "Forgive, forgive." And I will never forget my encounter with God right in my bedroom; it hit me like a ton of bricks. When I released that unforgiveness, I was immediately and totally set free and never returned.

And that is one of the reasons that I never talk about it. You would never see any of those traits in me with my own children. Sometimes when you hold unforgiveness, you will become the very thing that happened to you. Unforgiveness and offense do more harm to churches than anything else. People leave the church because of offense, and they never forgive. They are missing the purpose of God in their life. They stop themselves from operating in a true level of faith. They cannot receive everything God has for their life because of the blockage of unforgiveness in their heart.

## Ought, Be Removed, and Cast into the Sea

Now God said in Ezekiel 36:26, *A new heart also will I give you, and a new spirit will I put within you: and I will take away the stony heart out of your flesh, and I will give you an heart of flesh.* But we have to have the desire to walk in total forgiveness in every area of our life. Now some of us came out of the same kind of church that I did, and when we left, they sent us to Hell, didn't they? The way they treated us presented us the perfect opportunity to walk with ought in our hearts against them because they were supposed to be our brothers and sisters. Yet it turned out they were our enemy. We were ready to stone them, but we had to let go of those things. Some of us are carrying offenses and unforgiveness towards our spouses. You are living with them, but you haven't forgiven them. If you think the person that offended you will be the last one, think again. You can walk around all of your life full of unforgiveness, offense, and ought in your heart toward your brother. As a matter of fact, the Bible says if you have ought in your heart against your brother, you should approach them and talk to them about it (Matthew 5:24). You need to go and talk to them; do not let unforgiveness fester. We must act like adults and have adult conversations without letting emotions get in the way as if we were still children.

So, why do people leave the church and allow their spiritual walk to be hindered? They cannot overcome ought, offense, or unforgiveness. Do you know what holds us back from forgiving and getting over it? It is called pride. Pride to say you are sorry even when you think you are right. To ask for forgiveness even when you know you did nothing wrong. There must be another step other than saying, "I'm sorry." You need to say, "I need you to forgive me." Even when you think you are right, "Please forgive me." And then, ultimately, it is up to the other person to forgive you. We have to get our hearts right. Revival starts in the hearts of individuals, not in a church building. Your faith will not work with unforgiveness and ought in your heart.

As believers, we must realize that faith only works with hope, faith, and love, but most of all, with love. As a believer, you must operate out of love because faith cannot work without love. If you are operating in love, you are constantly forgiving. Do not complain, do not harbor ought in your heart. Instead, pray, speaking the Word. When counseling young ladies, my wife often says, "Instead of complaining about what your husband is or isn't doing, try confessing what you desire over him." Do not allow ought to penetrate your heart.

You can get offended and hold unforgiveness, or you can speak out your desires. John Bevier and his wife, Lisa, are founders of Messenger International Ministry. John spoke his wife into the speaker she is. He told her, "You are going to speak to the world just like me. You are going to preach, prophecy, speak the Word, and write books." Lisa is preaching all over the world just like him. He spoke it into existence. She has a prosthetic eye with which she was concerned. But he said, "You are going to do this." He kept speaking the Word of God into her life. Do not receive unforgiveness; speak what you desire. Instead of harboring unforgiveness in our hearts, we have to speak to the mountain of ought and say, "Be thy removed and cast into the sea." We must believe that it is gone when we command it to be removed from our hearts. Speak what you desire. Declare the Word of God!

There are people reading this who are offended and mad at God. You are still wondering, "Why did you let my marriage fall apart? Why did you let that happen to me when I was a child?" It is okay if you are mad at God. He is not worried because to be mad at someone, you have to actually believe in them. But once and for all, it must end. You do not have to carry unforgiveness in your heart. You do not have to carry that weight that continues to pull you down. Just forgive. Giving it all to the Lord is the easiest way to do that. Do what I did that day in my room. I said, "Lord, I give him to you. I give this offense to you and this unforgiveness to you. I lift him up to you, and I let it go. My father was an alcoholic, but today is the day that I drop the offense. I drop the offense and let all that unforgiveness out." Let it all out so that your faith can begin to work like a factory producing everything God has for you. A faith factory that manufactures exactly what you desire from God.

# CHAPTER 6

## *Faith on Fire:*
## The Voice of God

Every time Bishop Bill Godair and I would meet, I always brought a pen and a piece of paper. This is one of the things he said that I wrote down. He said, "There's nothing like a good understanding." If you can get a good understanding of the voice of faith, there will be nothing like it to elevate your faith to a higher level.

Matthew 12:33-37 declares:

Either make the tree good, and his fruit good; or else make the tree corrupt, and his fruit corrupt: for the tree is known by his fruit. O generation of vipers, how can ye, being evil, speak good things? for out of the abundance of the heart the mouth speaketh. A good man out of the good treasure of the heart bringeth forth good things: and an evil man out of the evil treasure bringeth forth evil things. But I say unto you, That every idle word that men shall speak, they shall give account thereof in the day of judgment. For by thy words thou shalt be justified, and by thy words thou shalt be condemned. (KJV)

The word *idle* translates to nonproductive or unfruitful. What kind of conversations do we have that are nonproductive or unfruitful? *Lay aside every nonproductive, unfruitful word that men shall speak, they will also give an account thereof on the Day of Judgment.* So this Scripture explains that we will be held accountable for every word we speak out of our mouths. *For by thy words thou shalt be justified and by thy words thou shalt be condemned.* Now let me add this. The Lord doesn't have to condemn you or judge you. You will judge and condemn yourself by what you speak out of your mouth. When the heart is not filled with the Word, the force of faith is not there. When the heart is not full of the Word, what we speak will not proceed, activate, or manifest into the natural. One thing we must understand when focusing on the believer's heart is that the heart cannot be full of the Word if it is filled with other things. We know the Word is the divine inspiration of God. We know that Jesus was the Word made flesh. We believe in the Word. We live by the Word; everything is by the Word. We do not have faith in the Word; we have faith in God. I don't literally mean we don't have faith in the Word, but it becomes a problem when we have faith in the Word and leave God out.

## Heart Transplant

I am going to nail this next subject down until there is a riot or revival. Either you will get upset, or you will receive a revelation, and God is going to do something in your life. But one of the two, we are going to get you there. I am determined to hammer this until you are no longer able to be offended. You have to have the ability to control your emotions. When we suffer bitterness, unforgiveness, rejection, abandonment, insecurities, or similar issues, we have no space in our hearts for the Word to manifest. You say, "Well, I have a big heart." No matter how big the heart, these issues take up all the space. You cannot be full of the Word and full of unforgiveness. For example, you cannot love God and be racist. You cannot have hate and love in your heart at the same time. You cannot hate a person because of the color of their skin or the accent of their language and say you love God. It is impossible.

Hate will take up everything on the inside of you. Unforgiveness will consume all the space in your heart, and the Word of God will not be able to penetrate it. Romans 10:17 says, *So then faith cometh by hearing, and hearing by the Word of God.* When you hear the Word and your heart is full of something else, you have a blockage that prevents you from receiving the Word. It just bounces off. Unforgiveness, bitterness, and offense disable you from receiving the truth. It disables you from receiving what God has for your life. You might need to book an appointment with the Great Physician and receive a Holy Ghost heart transplant.

## Look at the Big Picture

Believers have to save their energy for the battles that matter. Some people are completely burned out by the time they need faith. They have interacted in so many battles; they are too tired to exercise their faith. Faith is not their priority anymore. If we put faith at the top of our list, the other things fade away. Some battles dissipate on their own if we learn to walk away from them. Some people are too quick to jump into the battle. You have to save your energy for battles that matter. Romans 8:28 states, *And we know that all things work together for good to them that love God, to them who are the called according to his purpose.* We know God is working it out for our good, right?

Have you ever had your house remodeled? They start tearing down walls and ripping everything up. It can get pure chaotic. It is a mess. It can be very stressful. You have to stay focused on what the end result will look like. That is what life is like at times. We go through circumstances, and we are focusing on the rubble. How can you turn things around? It is like a puzzle. There are a thousand pieces, and when things are mixed up, it is confusing, but when those thousand pieces are in place, it is a beautiful thing.

When my wife is baking a cake, I don't even go in the kitchen because it looks like a tornado went right through it. It is a mess! If it is a double-layer cake, then it is double the mess. Triple cupcakes and pots and pans are everywhere. When someone takes a bite of her Reece's triple cupcake, they don't see all the messy stuff. Many times we look at somebody else, but we don't see all the stuff they are going through. You have to let that battle simmer and say, "Lord, what is the big picture? Sometimes I don't understand the big picture, but I know you have one. The way that person is treating me will somehow work for my good." Otherwise, you will go home mad, and it will rob you of all your energy. You could reserve that energy to create a business, ministry, means to get out of debt, or something for your kids that will last for generations. But no, we are spending too much time gossiping about everybody. We could be building something up every minute we occupy tearing someone down. We have to look at the big picture in our life. Every moment counts.

When you take the time to invest in gossiping about someone, not only are you nonproductive, but you are also picking up their offense. Do not give someone who is offended a microphone. Do not take on somebody else's offense. If you meditate on it long enough, it goes from your mind to your heart. You have to examine the motive of the conversation. Is your motive to bring them closer to Christ or bring yourself closer to Christ? You have to really search your heart and ask, "What is the motive?" You have to examine what you are thinking. You have to examine what you are speaking. Have you ever walked away and gotten this feeling in your stomach and said, "I shouldn't have said that; what was I thinking?" You must examine your heart and ask, "Is this faith?" Always speak the Word. Speak what matters. Do not throw away your time on this earth. Never have to look back and ask yourself, "What have I been doing for the last three years? Why have I wasted so much time on stupid stuff?" Do not use your energy or your words to talk about situations or conversations that are not productive. Save your energy for battles that matter. Learn to focus on the big picture.

## Refuse to Bow

When most people come to me for counseling, they just want me to agree with them. They have made their minds up. When our heart is filled with issues, and we are holding on to things of the past, we are creating a wall that stops us from receiving the Word. It disables us from receiving the Word when it is being released. Jesus said, "Out of the abundance of the heart the mouth speaks." So whatever is in the heart comes out of the mouth. Whatever is in the heart will be the product that produces the fruit. If bitterness is in the root, it will be in the fruit. Whatever is in the roots will manifest. When you are full of the Word of God, you will speak faith-filled words that dominate the law of death and all of its forces that the enemy has ruled since the fall of Adam. When you are full of the Word in your heart, you will respond with the Word. When Jesus was being tempted by Satan, what did he do? He responded with the Word. We have to respond with the Word of God in every situation of our life.

Romans chapter 8:2 says, *For the law of the Spirit of life in Christ Jesus hath made me free from the law of sin and death.* When we get the Word on the inside of us, and we start to confess the Word, we release the life of the Spirit into our situations and into the atmosphere. Remember, Jesus, has already set us free, as in the past tense. Whatever you are believing God for, He has already done it. You have to speak it into existence. We must refuse to bow our confessions to the law of death just as Shadrach, Meshach, and Abednego did in Daniel 3:17 and 25:

If it be so, our God whom we serve is able to deliver us from the burning fiery furnace, and he will deliver us out of thine hand, O king.

He answered and said, Lo, I see four men loose, walking in the midst of the fire, and they have no hurt; and the form of the fourth is like the Son of God. (KJV)

When our confession is right, we are refusing to bow to death's law. When we start confessing and speaking the Word, we say it doesn't matter if you throw me in a fire, it doesn't matter if you talk about me; it doesn't matter if you call my name down; it doesn't matter if you ruin my reputation, because it is not about my reputation, rather, it is about His reputation. You can lie on me, cheat on me, steal from me; you can do anything you want to me, but there is a fourth man standing with me in the fire. And whatever the enemy throws at me, it will not burn my clothes. It will not hurt my family. It will not hurt my finances. It will not hurt anything. But before Shadrach, Meshach, and Abednego could see it, they had to speak it out of their mouth, "God will deliver us. He is faithful to deliver us." They had to speak it before they could see it. They had to get their confession in line so the force of faith could come behind it and produce the fourth man in the fire.

So when your confession is right, that is when Jesus gets in your boat. When your confession is right, that is when God begins to move on your behalf and calm the seas that are raging in your life. He says, "Listen, if you speak my Word, I will watch over it to perform it." You have to speak it for Him to perform it. It is hard to speak the Word if you are speaking outside the Word. We shouldn't have any nonproductive conversations.

Daniel 3:27 said:

And the princes, governors, and captains, and the king's counsellors, being gathered together, saw these men, upon whose bodies the fire had no power, nor was an hair of their head singed, neither were their coats changed, nor the smell of fire had passed on them. (KJV)

Again, Daniel 3:17 said, *If it be so, our God whom we serve is able to deliver us...* This is what they are speaking to them. They spoke it out, and then God performed it. What are you going to speak this week for God to perform in your life? They spoke it out. The voice of faith was so powerful that God did not even allow fire to jack up their clothes. When they came out of the fire, they said, "We can't even smell the smoke on you." There was nothing wrong with them. There was no evidence they were in a fire. Every hair on their head looked good. They had to speak the voice of faith out of their mouth. If you cannot speak it out, it is not on the inside of you.

## The Authority of the Believer

As a believer, we have to exercise authority in the world of the spirit. How do you do that? Ephesians 2:10 states, *For we are his workmanship, created in Christ Jesus unto good works, which God hath before ordained that we should walk in them.* We can walk in the works of God. We are created in Christ. You have to believe that. You have to have faith in that. And then you have to speak it.

Colossians 1:13 says, *Who hath delivered us from the power of darkness, and hath translated us into the kingdom of his dear Son:* He translated us into His kingdom. We are born again. This is not what we do after we die and go to heaven. That is called escapism. We are not called to live until He Comes; the Bible says to occupy until he comes. *Occupy* means to do business transactions or to be productive and do business. He has delivered us, not so we can only celebrate when we get to heaven, but to experience the Kingdom of God right here on earth.

2 Corinthians 4 says: *Among them the god of this world [Satan] has blinded the minds of the unbelieving to prevent them from seeing the illuminating light of the gospel of the glory of Christ, who is the image of God* (AMP). Jesus, the body of Christ, and the angels dominate Satan and his demons in the world and the spirit world as well. You will never know what is available to you because the world will keep you blind. There is a system in this world designed to keep you dumb, blind, brainwashed, and dependent on somebody else. And it has nothing to do with which political side you are on. Besides, it is the same snake with two heads.

The gospel says you have authority through your faith and through what Jesus has done for you. You have an authority you can use, but you must realize that the world does not want you to have it.

The world does not want you to get a good understanding of Matthew 18:18-20 which says:

Verily I say unto you, Whatsoever ye shall bind on earth shall be bound in heaven: and whatsoever ye shall loose on earth shall be loosed in heaven. Again I say unto you, That if two of you shall agree on earth as touching any thing that they shall ask, it shall be done for them of my Father which is in heaven. For where two or three are gathered together in my name, there am I in the midst of them. (KJV)

How do you exercise your authority? Do you bind and loose? It is all by your words. There is nothing you can do in the natural. It is all about the words you speak out of your mouth. Whatever you bind in the physical realm will be bound in the heavenly realm. Whatever you loose in this physical realm will be loosed in the heavenly realm. Whatever you bind and loose will activate, change, and move situations in your life.

## Words Control Your Angels

God has also given you authority over angels. The Bible actually states that angels are under our authority.

Hebrews 1:5-14 declares:

For unto which of the angels said he at any time, Thou art my Son, this day have I begotten thee? And again, I will be to him a Father, and he shall be to me a Son?... But to which of the angels said he at any time, Sit on my right hand, until I make thine enemies thy footstool? Are they not all ministering spirits, sent forth to minister for them who shall be heirs of salvation? (KJV)

Who is the heir of salvation? You are the heir of salvation. 1 Corinthians 6:3 says, *Know ye not that we shall judge angels? how much more things that pertain to this life?* He is talking to you and me. Angels are ready to go and work for you because you are moving in the name of Jesus. You have been given authority in the Holy Ghost. They are ready to work for you. You say, "Well, what do you mean?" Revelation 1:1 says, *The Revelation of Jesus Christ, which God gave unto him, to shew unto his servants things which must shortly come to pass; and he sent and signified it by his angel unto his servant John:* Revelation is not a book of ghosts and goblins to scare you. It is actually the revelation of Jesus Christ. Matthew 18:10 explains, *Take heed that ye despise not one of these little ones; for I say unto you, That in heaven their angels do always behold the face of my Father which is in heaven.*

Angels are ready to work for you, but our confession controls their powers. Luke Chapter 12:8-9 declares, *Also I say unto you, Whosoever shall confess me before men, him shall the Son of man also confess before the angels of God: But he that denieth me before men shall be denied before the angels of God.* Whatever you confess, there is a voice in the heavens that echoes what you are saying, and when that voice echoes, your angels begin to move. They begin to move on your behalf. Say, "I have angels; I just have to learn how to talk to them." So when you confess in faith, they start moving. When you confess in faith, they start working.

## Build or Tear Down

All believers are carriers of faith. When Jesus lives inside of you, you are a walking vessel of faith. People in the world are looking to you for an answer. What does that mean for them if we fail in times of trouble? Proverbs 24:10 says, *If you falter in a time of trouble, how small is your strength!* I am not saying we have to be perfect and look like we have it all together. How can we speak negativity, doubt, fear, and gossip when we are a child of the living God? We are in the Kingdom of Light; people in darkness are looking at us for an answer. We have to examine ourselves. David often repeated in Psalms, *Examine my heart O Lord.* We have to make faith a priority. Examine your thoughts. We can live in faith all day long. We can be carriers of faith and operate on a supernatural level the whole day. I am not talking about being so heavenly-minded that you are no earthly good. But your mind has to be set above. Your affections are set above because you are a carrier of faith.

On a personal level, if my wife and I disagree, we do not speak about the disagreement to others, especially our family members. We cannot sow doubt into our family members about our spouse and then wonder

70

why they start treating them differently. You are only presenting your side. You do not want to talk negatively about your spouse to others. Why not? Guess what, you married them. You chose them. You will look ridiculous if you talk down on them. If I am talking about my spouse, guess who I am also talking about? Yes, me.

How often have you been mad about something and talked to somebody else? Through your confession, you were sowing idle words in their heart. You get over it; they do not. I learned long ago that if somebody talks negatively about your pastor, you better turn and run. It doesn't matter whether they have a case or not. Change the subject or run from the hell it will likely produce. Ask yourself, "Is this conversation productive?" That is a fundamental question. If it could actually cause someone to stumble in their faith, it would be better for you to have a millstone tied around your neck and be cast into the sea (Matthew 18:6). Is your conversation about His kingdom? Is it bringing someone closer to Christ? Is it building the Kingdom of God, or is it tearing the kingdom down? There are only two options. We build, or we tear down.

## The Voice of Our Confession

Hebrews 3:1 says, *Wherefore, holy brethren, partakers of the heavenly calling, consider the Apostle and High Priest of our profession, Christ Jesus.* He is the apostle and priest of our profession or confession. What are you speaking? Jesus Christ, the high priest of our confession. He is the voice of our confession in heaven. Psalms 103: 20 states, *Bless the LORD, ye his angels that excel in strength, that do his commandments, hearkening unto the voice of his word.* Did you read that, the voice of His Word? When you speak the Word, the angels harken to that. He echoes what you confess in the heavens. He is the high priest. He ensures that the voice of your confession is not hindered by distance. Our confession is the voice of His Word in the earth. When we confess the Word, we are speaking the words of God; therefore, the angels and heaven stand at attention. Everything in the earth stands at attention. Heaven is waiting for it. Ministering angels are waiting for it. He is saying, "If you just speak it, I will release it." But you will never speak it out of your mouth if it is not in your heart first.

That is why people are struggling with addiction. The worst thing they can do is speak, "I am never going to get over this; I am never going to get better; I am never going to get out of debt." No, if you speak the Word, you will change the circumstance. You can defeat it. Confess it; speak the Word over your children.

My brother was in prison, but my mom kept confessing the Word, "The seed of the righteous shall be delivered." They tried to send him to prison for twenty-eight years for drug trafficking. His sentence was reduced to four years in prison. Mom kept declaring, "The seed of the righteous shall be delivered." She continually confessed, "He will be a man of God; he will be what you have called him to be." She kept speaking it, even in the face of adversity where it looked like there was no chance. I want you to know he owns his own business today. He is established. He was saved within a year after he was released. He made six figures in his first year of business. We kept speaking and declaring. Even when it looks like it is worsening, you must keep speaking. When you speak, the force of faith is with you. Keep believing; keep speaking; keep confessing; keep declaring because God will bring it to pass, and He will move heaven and earth on your behalf. Jesus is the voice of our confession in heaven. He is the voice of our faith.

# Faith to Possess the Land

## Part II

# CHAPTER 7

## Faith to Possess the Land:
## The Spirit of Faith

I am going to start part two, *Faith to Possess the Land,* by building on the foundation of the voice of faith with the spirit of faith. 2 Corinthians 4:13 says, *We having the same spirit of faith, according as it is written, I believed, and therefore have I spoken; we also believe, and therefore speak.*

According to this Scripture, whatever we believe comes from our mouths. *According as it is written, I believed...* is in the past tense. For example, we believe the healing has already been done. We already believe we are walking in the fullness of what God has for our life, based on the finished work at Calvary. It is about believing and speaking; if you do not believe you can possess it, you will never possess it because you will never speak it or declare it out of your mouth. You have to believe that the house belongs to you. You have to believe that healing belongs to you. We have the same spirit of faith. The same spirit of faith believes; therefore, it speaks, and what it speaks, it receives. Believe, speak, and receive.

Romans 4:16-25 states:

Therefore it is of faith, that it might be by grace; to the end the promise might be sure to all the seed; not to that only which is of the law, but to that also which is of the faith of Abraham; who is the father of us all, (As it is written, I have made thee a father of many nations,) before him whom he believed, even God, who quickeneth the dead, and calleth those things which be not as though they were. Who against hope believed in hope, that he might become the father of many nations, according to that which was spoken, So shall thy seed be. And being not weak in faith, he considered not his own body now dead, when he was about an hundred years old, neither yet the deadness of Sarah's womb: He staggered not at the promise of God through unbelief; but was strong in faith, giving glory to God; (KJV)

## Truth Changes Facts

I want to talk about the difference between fact and truth. This is very important when we decide what we are called to say. A fact would be Abraham was old, right? He was very unlikely to bear a child. The truth is that God gave Abraham a promise that he would have descendants with Sarah. So faith is not denying the facts. Sometimes we get this a little twisted. Truth supersedes facts. Truth is God's Word, and it supersedes any fact in the natural. Facts change, but truth remains the same. So the spiritual law supersedes the natural law. God's promises supersede natural law. A fact is that Abraham was old, but God's promises superseded that. Let's use the law of gravity as an example. If I drop a ball, it will drop to the floor, right? That is the law of gravity. That is a natural law. What about the law of lift? How does an airplane take off? Does that mean the law of gravity is not true? The law of gravity is absolutely true, but the law of lift has superseded the law of gravity. So the truth of flying changes the facts of flying. Applied truth changes facts. When you speak the truth of God's Word, it changes the facts. We are not denying the facts; we are changing the facts. So faith calls things that are *not* as though they *were*. Thank you, Lord, for your Word that is superseding everything we see in the natural.

Romans 10:6-8 declares:

But the righteousness which is of faith speaketh on this wise, Say not in thine heart, Who shall ascend into heaven? (that is, to bring Christ down from above:) Or, Who shall descend into the deep? (that is, to bring up Christ again from the dead.) But what saith it? The word is nigh thee, even in thy mouth, and in thy heart: that is, the word of faith, which we preach; (KJV)

The Word has been sown into us. We listen to the Word being taught. We listen to the Word being preached. We listen to everybody's revelation of the Word. But do you know whose turn it is to speak it? Yes, mine. We can be around the Word all day long, but it must become mine. I have to speak that thing out. You can go to every conference from here to Africa, sit under the most prolific teaching, and then walk out and not speak it. It takes faith to speak the Word. We are not called to sit under it, but to be activators of it. We are called to speak it out of our mouths. Momma can't speak it out for us; Grandma can't speak it out for us. We have to speak it out for ourselves. By speaking the Word, we do not deny the facts; truth supersedes the facts. We declare those things that are *not* as though they *were*. You have to see it to speak it. You have to speak it to see it. God's ways are always higher than our ways.

## We Have the Title Deed

Genesis 1:26 says, *And God said, Let us make man in our image.* Let me interject a little doctrine here. The King James Bible actually mistranslates this Scripture. The word "us" is not plural. It does not mean more than one person. It is singular. *And God said, Let me create man in my own image, after my likeness: and let them have dominion...* The word *dominion* means the title deed. Man has the title deed over the fish of the sea, and over the fowl of the air, and over the cattle, and

77

over all the earth. *And over every creeping thing that creepeth.* So God gave you dominion over creeps (a little humor). Let's go back. God gave you the title deed. Have you paid your house off? When you pay your house off, they give you a title for that house. That means you are the sole owner. You own all of it. It belongs to you. Nobody can take it from you. They can't jack up the interest on you; it is paid off, and you are the sole owner. God gave us dominion. He created man and gave him the title deed over all the earth, and over every creeping thing that creepeth on the earth, so everything in this earth does not belong to the devil. It is the believer or the body of Christ who actually owns everything in this earth.

Here is the truth. You already own it, but you never showed up to collect it. God has already given you the title deed to the car you have believed for. What about that house or land that you are believing God for? Remember, He told Joshua in Chapter 1, *Everywhere the sole of your foot shall tread, you shall possess the land.* He will possess the land because God has already given him the papers to it, which is the confirmation and the title deed that proves it belongs to you. The following verses in Genesis 1:27-28 state, *So God created man in his own image, in the image of God created he him; male and female created he them. And God blessed them...* He gave you dominion, the title deed, and then he blessed you. You have to believe that you are the owner. The devil doesn't own anything. Do you believe the Word? He doesn't own anything... zero. Somebody said, "Well, the devil just has all things." You know the devil will lie to you because he told Jesus when he was tempted, "If you bow down and worship me I will give you all the nations of the world." He lied; he couldn't give him anything because he can't give something that doesn't belong to you.

Can you say, "I am blessed; I am blessed in the city; I am blessed in the field; I am blessed going in; I am blessed going out and everything I put my hands to is blessed." Why? Because he gave me the title deed and then turned around and blessed me. Then He said, "Be fruitful and multiply." He was not commanding you; He was promising you that you were going to be fruitful and multiply. You were going to replenish the earth and have dominion over it. That is God's plan for your life. It is His plan for you to exercise your faith, not just to have a little cabin over in glory land when you get to heaven.

This is God's plan of dominion rights for man. Isaiah 55:8-11 declares:

For my thoughts are not your thoughts, neither are your ways my ways, saith the LORD. For as the heavens are higher than the earth, so are my ways higher than your ways, and my thoughts than your thoughts. For as the rain cometh down, and the snow from heaven, and returneth not thither, but watereth the earth, and maketh it bring forth and bud, that it may give seed to the sower, and bread to the eater: So shall my word be that goeth forth out of my mouth: it shall not return unto me void, but it shall accomplish that which I please, and it shall prosper in the thing whereto I sent it. (KJV)

Notice it is not what you please but what God pleases. He has given you dominion. He has called you blessed. You are the head and not the tail. You are above and not beneath. You are blessed in the city and blessed in the field. I have called you to take territory and to occupy until I come… to do business. I have called you. The kingdom suffers violence, but the violent take it by force." God is saying, "Get out of your own head and get in your spirit so you can get a revelation that you are fighting for something that already belonged to you two thousand years ago." It has been paid for. You have to show up and collect it.

## Don't Wait on Your Ducks to Get in a Row

Are you scared to go look at the house? Are you scared to go get in the car and drive it? I hear people say, "I am going to wait till I get all my money." Or they say, "I am going to wait until I get married." Good luck. How about, "We are waiting until we have a baby." It doesn't work that way. We never make moves or walk in the possessions that are rightfully ours because we are waiting for something to manifest in the natural when it has already manifested in the spirit. It would not take faith if all our ducks were in a row. Bishop didn't start this church because he had all his ducks in a row or all the money in the bank. He did it out of what? He did it out of faith. So you have to start in faith, lean on the Word, and get out of your head and get in your spirit and say, "It doesn't matter how much money I have in the bank. It doesn't matter what is going on in my life. God said it. I believe it. I am pouring the water into the vessels, and it is His job to turn the water into wine. I will do my part by pouring the water, and God will supernaturally do His part."

What is your calling? Everybody is always asking me, "Why am I here? I answer, "To have dominion over it." You are swimming in it and still missing it. It is so simple you are missing it. You have been called to have dominion, to be blessed, replenish, and be fruitful on the earth.

1 Corinthians 1:26-27 explains:

For ye see your calling, brethren, how that not many wise men after the flesh, not many mighty, not many noble, are called: But God hath chosen the foolish things of the world to confound the wise; and God hath chosen the weak things of the world to confound the things which are mighty; (KJV)

God is no respecter of persons. It doesn't matter how many teeth you have in your head. It doesn't matter what your education is. If that were the case, then God would be a respecter of persons. It has nothing to do with your IQ level. It has to do with being a person driven by the Word and the principles of the Word. It doesn't matter if you have been addicted to heroin, alcohol, or anything else. You have been delivered. It doesn't matter what you have done in the past. God will use you. You do not have to be perfect; you just have to be willing.

That is what people are missing. I know that some people think I never do anything wrong, but my wife begs to differ. God uses the dirty things or the foolish things. The amplified says, *God uses filthy rags to confound the wise.* In the Book of Acts 4:13, they said, "We looked at these men and they were ignorant uneducated men," but they said, "You know what, we know that they've been with Jesus." It doesn't matter your education if you have been with Jesus. Everything changes when you have an encounter with the Lord. Here is another Scripture.

1 Corinthians 1:28-31 states:

And base things of the world, and things which are despised, hath God chosen, yea, and things which are not, to bring to nought things that are: That no flesh should glory in his presence. *[Faith only gives glory to God].* But of him are ye in Christ Jesus, who of God is made unto us wisdom, and righteousness, and sanctification, and redemption: That, according as it is written, He that glorieth, let him glory in the Lord. (KJV)

## I Got the Power

Everything we do is dependent on what Christ has already done. We do not perform works to get righteous. Good works are produced out of righteousness. The subject is dominion. How did Jesus use this dominion?

81

When we say Jesus uses God's dominion, we mean the humanity of God, how the humanity of God was being demonstrated in the earth.

Mark 1:40-42 states:

And there came a leper to him, beseeching him, and kneeling down to him, and saying unto him, If thou wilt, thou canst make me clean. And Jesus, moved with compassion, put forth his hand, and touched him, and saith unto him, I will; be thou clean. And as soon as he had spoken, immediately the leprosy departed from him, and he was cleansed. (KJV)

Let me emphasize this. Quit feeling sorry for people; have compassion for them. Feeling sorry and having compassion are two different things. Jesus didn't feel sorry for anybody. He had compassion for people. He tells him to be made clean. You have to tell your body to line up with the Word of God. You have to speak to your situation with authority and say, "I draw a line in the sand. I have dominion and authority in the name of Jesus. I command you to get in line in the mighty name of Jesus." And as soon as he had... what? Oh, you're talking about that *speaking it* stuff again. Immediately the leprosy departed from him, and he was what? He was healed.

As soon as Jesus spoke it, he was healed. There was no delay. When you are connected with your faith, supernatural things happen. How many of you believe the quantity of water in a lake is far greater than the quantity of water in a cup? When you get an entire church operating in this realm of faith, believing that when they speak, it is already done, they can turn their county upside down for the glory of God. Bishop told me that in Ethiopia, they do not pray for revival; they pray for unity. If you get in unity, you will have revival. We will see miracles, signs, and wonders if we come into unity and faith.

Luke 13:10-13 say:

And he was teaching in one of the synagogues on the Sabbath. And, behold, there was a woman which had a spirit of infirmity eighteen years, and was bowed together, and could in no wise lift up herself. And when Jesus saw her, he called her to him, and said unto her, Woman, thou art loosed from thine infirmity. *[So he spoke it first]* And he laid his hands on her: and immediately she was made straight, and glorified God. (KJV)

You have to speak it and lay your hands on it. The humanity of God is operating in that dominion. Have enough faith to speak it and lay hands on it. Call the realtor, walk in the house, walk on the property, sit in the car, and go test drive it. If you do not have faith to do that, God will not do his part. If you cannot even show up for the blessing, why should He give it to you? He spoke it and laid hands on her. Start laying hands on people. When I hold revival, I lay hands on everything until something moves. If it doesn't move, we keep laying hands on it until it does. We are going to get some results. There is going to be a revival or riot… one of the two.

In Mark 11:14, Jesus instructs, *And Jesus answered and said unto it, No man eat fruit of thee hereafter forever. And his disciples heard it.* Jesus is operating in such a level of dominion that he curses it the day before, and then the next day his disciples bring it to his attention. He never even turns and looks back at it because he knows it is already done. If you are speaking it and then constantly checking on it, you are not operating in that dominion. Jesus took care of it, and no man is ever going to eat from that thing again. It is done! He never even looks at it or gives it any more attention. He just keeps walking and talking.

John 11:1-4 says:

> Now a certain man was sick, named Lazarus, of Bethany, the town
> of Mary and her sister Martha. (It was that Mary which anointed the
> Lord with ointment, and wiped his feet with her hair, whose brother
> Lazarus was sick.) Therefore his sisters sent unto him, saying, Lord,
> behold, he whom thou lovest is sick. When Jesus heard that, he said,
> This sickness is not unto death, but for the glory of God, that the Son
> of God might be glorified thereby… These things said he: and after
> that he saith unto them, Our friend Lazarus sleepeth; but I go, that
> I may awake him out of sleep. (KJV)

Jesus is projecting through dominion that He has the power.
Alright, the same spirit that raised Christ from the dead dwells in
whom? The same spirit dwells in us. Jesus is saying, "I am going to
go. I am going to speak. And when I speak, that thing that is sleeping
will awaken." When he gets there, He calls him out by name. Do you
know that had He not called him out by name, He would have
resurrected the whole graveyard? He called him specifically by name.
Can you imagine the whole graveyard standing up? He calls him out.
He knew He had the authority. You and I are in Christ. We have the
authority; remember the title deed. We have all this authority but never
tap into it because we do not believe it belongs to us. Say, "I got the
power."

## Faith of Abraham

Jesus said, "I will go because I am going to wake him." Let me
interject; you are about to wake some things with your faith. Some desires
and dreams you have been sleeping on are getting ready to awaken in your
spirit. God says, "I am going to give you the faith to wake them up."
What about Abraham's faith? He gave God glory by calling those
things that are not as though they were.

Remember what 1 Corinthians 1:27-28 states:

God hath chosen the foolish things of the world to confound the wise; and God hath chosen the weak things of the world to confound the things which are mighty; And base things of the world, and things which are despised, hath God chosen, yea, and things which are not, to bring to nought things that are: (KJV)

God is telling you to stop looking at your status and start calling those things that are *not* as though they *were*. You are worried about what is going on. You are trying to get all your ducks in a row. You are worried about having all the money. You are busy worrying, and you are missing the big picture. Stop majoring in the minor issues and start speaking where you desire to go.

Romans 4:19-21 declare:

And being not weak in faith, *[you can't be weak in faith]* he considered not his own body now dead, when he was about an hundred years old, neither yet the deadness of Sarah's womb: He staggered not at the promise of God through unbelief; but was strong in faith, giving glory to God; And being fully persuaded that, what he had promised, he was able also to perform. (KJV)

It was not just about him being old but also about his wife's womb; she could not conceive a child. Those were the facts. But the truth supersedes the facts. He was old, and she could not conceive. There was no way possible on either side of the spectrum that anything was going to manifest. But Abraham was strong in his faith. Your faith will always defile what it looks like in the natural. The enemy wants you sad, depressed, and feeling sorry for others and yourself. Stop being a victim; get up and be the victor. Knock the dust off your pants and declare, "In my weakness, He is strong. I am strong in the Lord and the power of His might. I have the faith of Abraham. Although it looks impossible in the natural, all things are possible with God."

In Genesis 22:5, Abraham said, *And Abraham said unto his young men, Abide ye here with the ass; and I and the lad will go yonder and worship, and come again to you.* He defied the odds with faith. He spoke faith. He was strong in his faith. God was saying, "You are going to sacrifice him." But when he is about to tell Isaac, Isaac says, "Dad, where's the sacrifice? You have the wood, the knife, and the fire. And Abraham said to him, "Son the Lord will provide the sacrifice." He spoke it before he could see it.

## Deep Cleaning

Let's go step by step on how to activate this faith that will possess the land every single day of your life. We are called to take territory every single day. You have to go to the Word to cover your situation. Have you ever played darts? The idea is to hit the bullseye. We can't patty cake it in life. If we are struggling with something, we must have an exact Scripture which deals with the situation. We have to take the Word and hit the bullseye instead of going around town, getting advice from everyone, and missing the mark. If we are not allowing that precise Scripture to rise up inside of us and fight off our negative thoughts, we are doing ourselves an injustice. We need the exact weapon to take down that thought.

I am a clean freak. In order to clean out all the dust that has been stored up for years, we have to move the furniture because that is where all the dust hides, right? Likewise, we have thoughts that hide in our hearts for years. Often these thoughts are repeated throughout generations. We never realized that there are things we learned as a kid that do not align with the Word of God. We have to deep-clean our hearts. We have to examine every thought and say, "I do not care what I have been thinking for the last ten, twenty, or forty years; this thought does not align with Scripture. I am not speaking that thought out loud. Speaking that thought would not be operating in my dominion. That would not be taking authority. That is not a victorious mentality." We have to deep-clean that thought out. We must move the furniture, even if we do not want to, and get it all out. It is hard work but worth the results. Then we must keep the Word before our eyes, ears, and mouths.

## The Best Defense is Offense

We live in a society that targets us with marketing twenty-four hours a day, seven days a week. We do not realize it because we are so accustomed to it. Constant commercials are programming our identity. We do not realize the effect it has on our minds. But we have the mind of Christ. We are who God says we are. I don't care who our friends tell us we are. I don't care who a counselor says we are. We are who God says we are. We have to be proactive, not reactive. We know this from sports. The best defense is a good offense. Many of us wait until we get in a situation, and then we go to the Word. No, we must remain full of the Word. We must possess the Word in our ears, mouths, and eyes to prepare us to face the adverse circumstances of life when challenges arise. You have to be prepared in season and out of season. The situations that used to stop us, knock us down, discourage us, or cause us anxiety, can no longer affect us. You know what you are going to do because you know where you are going. We are on the offense because the best defense is offense.

The devil has only so many tricks. I'm like, "Is that all you got? Are you firing that same dart again?" I already know what I am going to say to that one because it tends to be the same things or the same people. They have been the same demons since the beginning of time. Demons don't reproduce. You have to get an aggressive mentality and say, "You know that co-worker who gets on my nerves every single day, and I know it will probably happen again today, but this is how I will respond. I am going to find a Scripture about walking in love and start quoting it. I am attacking this situation." If you always get offended at church, just plan on the fact that you are going to get offended but don't allow yourself to fall for it. Or, if you know that your spouse will do something to offend you, expect to be offended, but refuse to be offended. Plan on it. Expect it, and do not act surprised. Instead, get ahead of it. Get aggressive with it. Get victory over it.

## Run the Red Light

We go to God based on His provision, not our needs. When God has already given us the vision, we can't sit around waiting for the provision. That would be like sitting at a traffic light when the light is green. The provision only comes when you start the vision. Usually, if God calls us to walk in faith, the provision comes after we start walking in the vision. It doesn't come before. I have never met anyone walking in divine faith that received all the money they believed for just sitting at the green light. You always hear someone proclaiming, "We signed the contract and didn't have the money, and the next day we got it!" When God says go, you have to go and trust Him for the provision to carry out your vision. If you trust Him, nothing can stop you. It is time to buckle up and put the pedal to the metal and run right through that red light, so to speak.

We have to go forward with the vision before the provision comes. Whatever God puts in your heart, when you hear His voice, you have to walk in it and speak to it.

1 Samuel 17:45-46 states:

Then said David to the Philistine, Thou comest to me with a sword, and with a spear, and with a shield: but I come to thee in the name of the LORD of hosts, the God of the armies of Israel, whom thou hast defied. This day will the LORD deliver thee into mine hand; and I will smite thee, and take thine head from thee; and I will give the carcasses of the host of the Philistines this day unto the fowls of the air, and to the wild beasts of the earth; that all the earth may know that there is a God in Israel. (KJV)

When the storms of life come, and the winds are raging, it is not the time to go and consult with all your friends who are doubters that cannot even receive their own victory. It is time to look straight in the enemy's face and declare goodness and victory in the name of Jesus. It is not the time to get everybody else's opinion. When God has called you to do something great, people will not agree with you or believe you ninety-nine percent of the time anyway. We have the Word of God that can defeat the enemy. That is why we have a David and Goliath story in the Bible (1 Samuel 17). David exercised tremendous faith. The testimonies do not come when times are easy, and everything is hunky dory. Our testimony is our greatest weapon. Put your foot on the pedal and floor it. God will give us the provision, and we will have a testimony. We can proclaim how the Lord delivered us through our trials and how we overcame our enemy by the blood of the Lamb and the word of our testimony (Revelation 12:11). Praise the Lord!

Praise is an expression of faith. Many Christians do not fully understand the place praise holds in receiving the answer to prayer. You can gauge the level of a person's faith based on the level of their praise. Prayer mixed with faith and praise produces results. You must praise God as if it has already been done. Don't pray, and pray, and pray about it. Praise him and begin to thank Him because it is done. It is finished. It is signed, sealed, and delivered. He has already performed it. Receive it and praise His mighty name. Hallelujah! Thank you, Jesus!

# CHAPTER 8

*Faith to Possess the Land:*
## Put Your Foot on It

You have to go and put the sole of your foot on the land that you want to possess. Put your faith into action.

Joshua 1:1-9 declares:

Now after the death of Moses the servant of the LORD it came to pass, that the LORD spake unto Joshua the son of Nun, Moses' minister, saying, Moses my servant is dead; now therefore arise, go over this Jordan, thou, and all this people, unto the land which I do give to them, even to the children of Israel. Every place that the sole of your foot shall tread upon, that have I given unto you, as I said unto Moses. From the wilderness and this Lebanon even unto the great river, the river Euphrates, all the land of the Hittites, and unto the great sea toward the going down of the sun, shall be your coast. There shall not any man be able to stand before thee all the days of thy life: as I was with Moses, so I will be with thee: I will not fail thee, nor forsake thee. Be strong and of a good courage: for unto this people shalt thou divide for an inheritance the land, which I sware unto their fathers to give them. Only be thou strong and very courageous, that thou mayest observe to do according to all the law, which Moses my servant commanded thee: turn not from it to the right hand or to the left, that thou mayest prosper withersoever thou goest. This book of the law shall not depart out of thy mouth; but thou shalt meditate therein day and night, that thou mayest observe to do according to all that is written therein: for then thou shalt make thy way prosperous, and then thou shalt have good success. Have not I commanded thee? Be strong and of a good courage; be not afraid, neither be thou dismayed: for the LORD thy God is with thee whithersoever thou goest. (KJV)

Romans 10:17 says, *So then faith cometh by hearing, and hearing by the word of God.* Hebrews 11:1 says, *Now faith is the substance of things hoped for, the evidence of things not seen.* I love the Book of Joshua because it demonstrates people moving out of one season into another. They are moving from a season of deliverance into a season of possession. You cannot continue trying to be delivered from something and possess something new at the same time. God has already brought you out through what He did for you on the cross at Calvary. You have already been delivered. As you move forward in your walk with the Lord, you must quit trying to get there and realize that you are already at that place to receive what he has for your life due to what Christ did on the cross. Many of us spend our lives trying to sit in a place where we are already seated. The Bible declares that you are seated in heavenly places with Christ Jesus (Ephesians 2:6). Why are you still trying to sit there if God has already sat you there? Our mindset must change from *we are being delivered* to *we have been delivered.*

I always tell people that if you have a sin consciousness, you will always produce sin in your life. But if you have a revelation of what has been accomplished at Calvary, you will not worry about having a sin conscious because you will know your sin has already been dealt with at the cross. You are not a sinner; you were a sinner. You have been saved by grace, and now you are the righteousness of God in Christ Jesus. It is not that the devil has ahold of you; you just haven't switched from being delivered to walking in the place of possession. You need to realize that you are not the person you used to be; you have been delivered. God does not need to get you out of what He delivered you from over two thousand years ago. God says, "I am trying to get you where I have called you; I am trying to get you to your purpose. I am trying to get you in your destiny. I am trying to get you to the place where you can rule and reign with me. I do not need to get you out. I need to get you into something because if I ever get you into it, the devil will not be able to stop my hand from moving and my plans unfolding in your life."

## The Little Foxes that Spoil the Vine

There has to be a mentality change if you are going to possess the land. You have to move out of the old and into something new. In order to do that, you have to learn to move beyond the issues. Some things are just a part of life; our biggest mistake is that we major in the minor things. We get stuck on a molehill and turn it into a mountain. We do not possess our land because we are mentally occupied with things that do not matter. I do not know about you, but I have recognized that God has called me. He has appointed me and anointed me. I do not have time to deal with issues that will never amount to a hill of beans. I do not have time for insignificant issues to occupy my mind. I do not have time to allow circumstances to hold me up. I am going somewhere. God is calling me higher, and I am not about to allow shallow-minded people or minor situations and challenges to hold me back from walking in the blessings that God has for my life and my family's future.

We spend most of our time fighting unnecessary things, which certainly will not produce fruit in our lives; therefore, the enemy is occupying and holding us hostage. We are stranded in a hallway and cannot discern which door to go through because we are occupied with something that doesn't matter. But when you are marked with purpose, have a higher calling, and begin to operate in faith, you are no longer held hostage by insignificant things. You are confessing, "I have too much invested. I have cried too much. I have given too much. I have praised God too much. I have prayed too much to let you stop me from moving into what God has for my life. I am brushing this thing off. I am getting beyond the issues. I am moving forward because God has a plan, and I will not let these little things mess it up." The Song of Solomon 2:15 reveals, *The little foxes, that spoil the vines...* The foxes are the little things you give attention to that really do not matter.

## It Pays to Believe

At the end of the day, it does not matter what they said or what they did. God loves you, and He has a plan for you. He marked you with his glory, and He wants you to get out of what people think and get in faith. Trust Him because He has something far greater for you than man can give you. It takes faith to look beyond current states and seasons. It takes faith when your banking account is empty, and you don't feel like looking at the house God has for you. It takes faith when everything around you appears to be falling apart, and everyone is sick. You are complaining, "God, but everybody's sick, and it looks like things are getting worse." It takes faith to look beyond current situations and circumstances and confess, "I will lift my eyes to the hills because that is where my help cometh from... the Lord." My help doesn't come from man. My help doesn't come from the government. My help doesn't come from the people around me. My help comes from the Lord. Some may trust in horses, others may trust in chariots, but I will trust in the name of God Almighty!

Give him praise. If I have the name, I have everything. If I have the name of Jesus, I have power over sickness and disease. I have power over lack. I have power over anything that the enemy can plant in my life to destroy me because if I have the name, I have everything. It pays to believe God while everyone else is living in doubt and wondering, "Lord, how is it all going to happen?" God always seems to send the Ravens to the people who trust Him. He will send them when everybody else is suffering, even during a pandemic. He will send the blessing to you because you believe that God is your source. Man is not your source. Nothing else is your source. Believe that payday is about to come into your house because it literally pays to believe.

## Faith Makes the Impossible Possible

When God is speaking to Joshua, He keeps repeating himself because he is developing confidence within Joshua and the people of Israel. God is already referring to them as the people of Israel, and they have yet to stand in their promised land physically. He will always call you victorious before it manifests in the natural. God has already called you healed. He has already called you delivered. He has already called you those things that are *not* as though they *were*. He keeps speaking to Joshua, "Have courage; have confidence; be strong." He keeps repeating it. Remember, confidence and faith are one and the same. If you have confidence in something, you also have faith in it. How many of you are confident in what you do? You have been doing it long enough that you are confident in your ability to do it. It is the same way with faith. When you are confident in something, you have faith in it. When you have faith in something, you are confident in it. God is not a man that He should lie. If He said He was going to do it, He is not going to let you down. He might not do it the way you want, but He will do it because He is a rewarder of those who diligently seek Him (Hebrews 11:6).

Faith and confidence activate the anointing in your life. When someone asks, "What is the anointing? I answer, "The ability of God within you to produce results out of you." Genesis 1:26 states, *I will create man in my*

95

*own image and he will have dominion over the face of the earth...* How many of you know that God is the creator? He is the creator of all things. If the same spirit that raised Jesus from the dead is in you, that same spirit also enables you to create. Your faith activates the ability of God within you to create or produce what God produces. It will always manifest in the spirit before it manifests into the natural. It has to manifest in your faith before it will ever manifest out into the natural realm. When you are operating in faith, you are operating under the influence of the Holy Ghost and out of the ability to bring what seems impossible to possible.

## Putting My Foot on It

I will never forget how the pandemic affected everything. Like everyone else, I was a little concerned about how it would play out. All the crazy people were getting crazier. According to history, there have been terrible diseases, such as Spanish Flu, but I have never experienced anything like this in my life. I just turned off all the news channels and began to seek the face of the Lord. I talked to the Lord and said, "I know that I am your son, and I know you feed the birds of the air; neither do they sew nor reap. How much more do you care for me?" The Lord said, "Brandon, I want you to buy a house." I said, "Lord, we're in the middle of a pandemic. Why would I buy a house right now?" He said, "Go buy a house." When you possess the land with faith, you have to get out of a renter's mentality. You have to get out of that mindset if you are going to possess the land. The Lord said, "I've put too great of an anointing on your life. I have blessed you too much for you to rent the rest of your life. But I said, "Lord, we are in the middle of a pandemic; what if it all falls apart?" He said, "I am your source, and I will sustain you just as I did Isaac in a famine" (Genesis 26:1-14). I woke up the next morning and told Tara, "We are going to buy a house." She said, "Now?" I said, "Yeah, we are going to buy a house."

I began thinking and processing everything. First, we started looking at virtual tours. Then we started looking around in the neighborhoods but did not see anything we liked. I called a realtor and told her exactly what I wanted. I told her exactly what I wanted to pay, how many bedrooms, and how many square feet because I had prayed about it and knew exactly what I wanted. She got on her computer, started pulling up houses, and showed us this brand-new neighborhood that was only seventy percent completed. She sent me some links, and I started looking at them and knew in my spirit that this was the community the Lord wanted us to live in. I just knew it. I said to my wife, "This is it." My wife agreed in her spirit that this was the community.

We pulled into the neighborhood, got out of the car, and this guy showed us some house models. We looked at the first one, and I said, "Nope, this is not it. This is not the one." He showed us another model, and my wife said to me, "This is it. This is the one." As soon as she said it, I felt it in my spirit and agreed, "You are right; this is the one." I told the guy, "I need to get qualified for it." He explained, "They will call you on the phone; because of the pandemic, they are qualifying over the phone." I sat on the couch, propping my feet up like I was living in it, and waited for them to call me. They finally called me back, asked me all these questions, and concluded, "Well, you are good to go; you are pre-qualified." I asked, "Is that it?" They responded, "Yeah, that's it." The ball was rolling, and I said, "I want this house," and the guy on the phone said, "I don't think that model is available. I think it is under contract." I said, "No, I know it's my house." Just like that, I claimed, "It's my house." He goes, "Well, I have to call them." He called them, and they figured out that the people buying it backed out. Of course, they did because it was my house, not theirs. The next day we received a call. They were doing a promotion, so we got an interest rate of 2.5 percent. He called us the next day and said, "You know, we were going to give you $8,000 for your closing cost, but your realtor talked to us, and now we are going to give you $12,000." I said, "Thank you very much."

My wife and I would go to that house every day because you know how those underwriters play it to the end. We would walk around in the house, and I would stand there and say, "Lord, wherever the sole of my foot shall tread, I will possess the land." I would walk around in the house. They were still building it. I knew it was that house, even though they had only laid the foundation. We wanted a corner lot; it was the neighborhood's largest yard and within a gated community. I would proclaim, "This is the one." My wife would confess, "This is our lot." We kept walking around in it, and the underwriters kept putting us off. We were pre-qualified, but they waited until the last minute before telling us everything worked out. They drag it out and make you think it is your fault. They would throw some ridiculous stuff at me because I had multiple streams of income coming in. They saw that I had bought an expensive watch and wanted to know why I needed the watch. I got so irritated; I asked the lady if she wanted a DNA sample. But I kept walking my feet on that property and would constantly confess, "Everywhere the sole of my foot shall tread, I will possess the land." Lord, your Word said it, and I believe it. You are not a man that you should lie; if you said it, it will come to pass. I would go over to sit in the house for thirty minutes at a time and answer phone calls because it was already my house. People might think I am crazy, but I spoke it before it was ever physically on the paper.

## Prayer Cannot Substitute Obedience

That is what faith does. It puts feet on it. People pray for a new car, but they are scared to go to the lot and put their feet on it. They pray for a new house, but will not go look at it, put their feet in the house, and get on their knees, saying, "God, you told me wherever the sole of my foot shall tread, I will possess the land. It doesn't matter what it looks like in the natural. If God said it in His Word, and it is His plan for your life, there is not a devil in hell that can stop the purpose of God in my life." Pick up your foot and put it down, repeating, "Lord, everywhere the soul of my foot shall tread, you have promised me that I will possess the land." We are going to possess the land everywhere we go. We will possess the land in the city, the county, the state, the country, and the world. We will possess the land from the Kingdom of Darkness and bring it into the Kingdom of Light. If the devil sticks his head up, we are going to put our foot on his neck, in the name above every name, the name of Jesus!

Let me add this. Prayer cannot substitute obedience. Many people are praying for revival, but maybe God is waiting for someone to act on revival, to start casting out devils and praying for the sick. That is how revival will start. You have to go out into the world. You cannot just pray and believe the Word; you have to obey it. You have to act on the Word. Faith without works is dead. Go, and you will possess it! Obey His commandment and go in obedience to the Word. He will make your way prosperous, and you will receive a double portion of prosperity over your life. When the spirit of prosperity hits your life, people that want to tell you *no* will have to say *yes*.

## God Sent the Memo

I was in Baton Rouge attending a ministry conference. I had been up all night traveling. I went to eat breakfast at the hotel. When I finished, I asked the lady serving my breakfast for the check, and she said, "No. Don't worry about it. While you were sitting here, I felt I couldn't charge you and that I needed to pay for it. I said, "Ma'am, please don't do that." She said, "There is something different about you. When you walked in here, I felt something. I can't charge you. I just can't." So she paid for it out of her own pocket. I left a twenty-dollar bill as a tip. Well, I went the next morning, and I had a male server. He says, "Sir, I don't know you, but I can't charge you. I want to bless you with breakfast today. You just look like a man of God." I confirmed, "I am a man of God." I said, "Lord, they must have received your memo at this restaurant.

## Put Your Feet on It

I am telling you, when you begin to operate out of faith and obedience, the Lord will cause the world to come and lay their treasures at your feet like they did in the Book of Acts. They laid it at the apostle's feet, and they will lay it at your feet. The wealth of the wicked is laid up for the righteous (Proverbs 13:22). When you get beyond the minor issues of life and begin to take courage to move forward with confidence and go put your feet on it, your faith will also increase. A lot of times, we are waiting to feel something or see something. You are waiting to get your ducks in a row, but I have news for you, they are never going to be in a row. You have to do it in faith. Faith it until you make it. Not fake it, but faith it because God is in the faith business, not faking business.

There are blessings you are waiting on, but God will not give them to you until you go and put your feet on it. If you have faith to put your feet on it, He says, "I will give it to you." Put your feet on it. It might sound ridiculous, but throw your debt on the floor and put your feet on it. God will give you a creative idea to completely wipe that debt out so you can live free. No believer is called to live in debt. We are the lender, not the borrower. You have to go and put your feet on it. You will be amazed. God will give you a creative miracle to pay it in full because if it is His will, it is His bill.

I believe as you read this, you are going to receive a supernatural increase in your faith. The Bible talks about transferring the gift of faith, which is called "the impartation." Something is going to ignite in your life. You are not going to be held back any longer by what you are seeing in the natural. You are not going to be moved when you hear a bad report. You will just keep driving and smiling like nothing ever happened because you know you have been granted the victory. No person will be able to stop it. No devil can stop it. You will have your foot on it, and you will possess your land.

# CHAPTER 9

## Faith to Possess the Land:
## The Gift of Faith

Let's review. In Joshua 1:1-9, God tells Joshua that His servant Moses is dead. He told Joshua that the same promise He had given to Moses would extend to him. He also told Joshua to take courage, move forward, have confidence, and have faith that wherever the soul of his foot shall tread, he will possess the land. When we read this in the Old Testament, we have to understand that when God spoke to Joshua, it was the end of an old order and the beginning of a new order. He was bringing them out of a season of being delivered and into a season where they would begin to possess what always belonged to them.

Romans 10:12-17 declare:

For there is no difference between the Jew and the Greek: for the same Lord over all is rich unto all that call upon him. For whosoever shall call upon the name of the Lord shall be saved. How then shall they call on him in whom they have not believed? and how shall they believe in him of whom they have not heard? and how shall they hear without a preacher? And how shall they preach, except they be sent? as it is written, How beautiful are the feet of them that preach the gospel of peace, and bring glad tidings of good things! *[So people who preach religion and legalism have ugly feet, but those who preach good tidings, have beautiful feet]* But they have not all obeyed the gospel. For Esaias saith, Lord, who hath believed our *report? So then faith cometh by hearing, and hearing by the word of God.* (KJV)

Galatians 3:22-26 states:

But the Scripture hath concluded all under sin that the promise by faith of Jesus Christ might be given to them that believe. But before faith came, we were kept under the law, shut up unto the faith which should afterwards be revealed *[the resurrection]*. Wherefore the law was our schoolmaster to bring us unto Christ, that we might be justified by faith. But after that faith is come, we are no longer under a schoolmaster *[under the law]*. For ye are all the children of God by faith in Christ Jesus.

## Out with the Old, In with the New

Moses represents a type of shadow type in the old covenant or living under the law. The name Joshua comes from the word *Yehoshua* which is the same as Jesus. It represents living under a new order, a new kingdom, or a new covenant. We have to understand that when Christ vacated heaven and came to earth, put on a bodysuit, and became the humanity of God, who knew no sin and died on the cross, He ended the old order or old covenant and established the new covenant so that you and I could also begin to walk in the dominion and authority that was established in Genesis 1:26. He said that the law got us to where we are but the law cannot take us to where He is calling us. The law got you to the altar, but the law cannot get you into your purpose or calling.

Paul writes in Galatians, "Look, you came in this one way but you have been delivered from the law. The only way you will possess the land is through faith by grace." When we are possessing the land, we are operating through faith. He said it is by the gift of faith that has been given to you. We understand this as we begin to operate under the new covenant. Regarding doctrine and belief, most people believe a little bit of the old covenant, a little bit of the new covenant, and a little bit of their own covenant. We have to understand the significance of the cross. When Jesus died on the cross, He established the New Covenant. The law no longer binds us; we are under grace, and that grace is through faith. That grace says, "Yes, you are worthy, yes you do have a calling, yes you are a child of God." It doesn't matter how badly you messed up; you have to get back up because what you did in the past cannot cancel out God's *yes* in your life.

We often beat ourselves up for what we committed instead of just receiving forgiveness by faith and saying, "Lord, your grace is sufficient for me." The word sufficient means more than enough. Your grace never runs out. It never goes dry. It is always enough. It reaches to the highest height; it goes to the lowest valley. Wherever I am, His grace will find me, and I have the faith to stand and say, "Listen, I might have done that, but that is not who I am because, in faith, I am the righteousness of Christ Jesus. I have been raised up in heavenly places. I am seated with him. I am the head and not the tail. I am above and not beneath. I am blessed in the city; I am blessed in the field. I am blessed going in; I am blessed going out." God didn't call me to sit here in the mud of my sin. He said, "Rise up in the name of Jesus and go get what belongs to you."

## When the Rope Ends, Faith Begins

I know that there is something out there that belongs to me. I know that God has called me to a higher place. I know He has a bigger purpose. God didn't raise me up to wash dishes for the rest of my life. He didn't raise me up to struggle and to pinch pennies. There is something greater. Every believer has been given a measure of faith when they come under the cover of the New Covenant. Faith comes even when you are not feeling it. As a matter of fact, it has nothing to do with your feelings. Remember, faith it until you make it. A lot of times, you can't go by your feelings, "Well, I'm just not feeling this. I'm not feeling that." Listen, when you are operating in faith, your emotions and senses will say, "No, stay where you are. This is just how it's going to be," but faith says, "Listen, I will not go by sight. I will not go by what I hear. I will not go by what I feel. I am going to rise up in the mighty name of Jesus. I am going to receive everything that God has for me." You might be tired, but you have faith. You might be beaten down, but you still have faith. You might feel like the world is crashing in, but I prophesy that faith is rising up on the inside of you. You might be at the end of the rope, but I'm telling you, when the rope ends, faith begins to arise, and God begins to do miracles, signs, and wonders.

When does faith come? It comes to whosoever will. Mark 11:23 says, *For verily I say unto you, that whosoever shall say*... So faith comes to those who will open their mouth. Faith is the same as possession. Possession will come when you start declaring that it is already yours. Who can speak it out of their mouth? Whoever will say, "I'll never be broke another day in my life? Come on, say it, "I'll never be broke another day in my life. I'll never be sick another day in my life. I'll never be poor another day in my life." God your Word says, "Whoever shall say it and believe it, shall have it." We declare that debts are going to be gone, houses are going to be built, and new cars are going to be driven off the lot because we believe it, we speak it, and therefore we receive it by faith.

## The Gift of Faith

Romans 12:3 says, *For I say, through the grace given unto me, to every man that is among you, not to think of himself more highly than*

106

*he ought to think; but to think soberly, according as God hath dealt to every man the measure of faith.* This is not talking about confidence; it is talking about people who depend on their own works without relying on the grace of God. He has given every man that calls upon the name of the Lord and is saved, which means every believer, a measure of faith when he is converted. So stop doubting yourself and asking yourself if you have faith. Ephesians 2:8 says you already have it. *For by grace are ye saved through faith; and that not of yourselves: it is the gift of God:* Oh, you mean dressing with a tie every day, shaving my face, and my wife growing her hair down to her ankles with no make-up doesn't save me? I said it. Do you mean all my righteous so-called works don't save me? Righteous works will not save you; it is grace that saves you. And when grace saves you, righteous works are the product of you being saved by grace. For by grace, you are saved through what? Faith, not of yourself. It is a gift from God.

When I teach this, people will ask, "Are you telling me that God gives man faith as a gift?" Not only will He save you, but He will empower you through faith. He gives you a gift of faith to receive what you want. If a believer has a gift of faith and operates in that gift, they also have the ability to impart the gift of faith through the impartation of laying on of hands. When a person is operating under the gift of faith, they have the ability to impart what is in them. The same gift of faith that is on the minister can also be on those who are under the sound of his voice. Everybody has it, but it takes the impartation to activate it.

II Thessalonians 3:2 says, *And that we may be delivered from unreasonable and wicked men: for all men have not faith.* Only the believer has the gift of faith. The world does not possess the ability to have faith. They can't receive it. As a matter of fact, the Bible says you were dead in your sins, and He called you into the marvelous light. He also said you didn't choose him, but he chose you. God had to resurrect you before you could even respond. Have you ever been to a graveyard and called out someone, and they responded to you? If so, you are in trouble because they are supposed to be dead. You cannot respond to the things of God until He calls you. If you are dead in your sins, how do you spiritually have any life in you? But when you are resurrected, and He calls you into the marvelous light, He also imparts the gift of faith within you, and that is your tool to walk and live your life as a believer and to receive everything God has for your life. So only the reborn have faith.

## Eat the Word to Grow Your Faith

How does our faith increase? Romans 10:17 says, *So then faith cometh by hearing, and hearing by the word of God.* He gives you a measure of faith, but He has also called you to build your faith. He gives you the foundation of it. He says I am going to give you a foundation, and it is your job to build it. Now listen, faith grows out of the Word; faith does not grow by praying for it. What do you mean? Prayer doesn't make faith work. Faith makes prayer work. Prayer does not make your faith work. Your faith makes your prayers work. Your faith cannot increase if you are not digesting the Word or getting the Word on the inside of you.

In John 6:56, Jesus said to the disciples, *He that eateth my flesh, and drinketh my blood, dwelleth in me, and I in him.* Jesus is the Word made flesh. He said, "You have to eat me, and you have to drink me. Don't leave out the eyes, the ears, or the tongue. You have to eat the whole cake and drink all of me if you are going to get it." And you can't eat all of it just on Sunday either. Eating just on Sunday will only get you through when the storm comes, and the winds rage. We have to eat the Word to grow our faith in God. God said, "I'll never leave you; I'll never forsake you. I am your waymaker. I am your miracle worker. I am your promise keeper. I will never let you down. I am God and a rewarder of those who diligently seek me." So our faith only increases when we begin to eat of Him.

Communion is not just a little cup of juice and a little piece of bread. People get stressed out if you don't observe the communion ordinance enough. It is actually about you being in communication with God. It is about you being in His Word on a daily basis. You can have communion three, four, or five times a day if you want. You can have communion all day if you want. You can have communion every day or every other day if you want. You can have communion anytime you want. It is communicating and talking with God. He says, "When you get in my Word, you are eating my flesh and drinking of my blood.

Faith causes prayer to work. It is important to stop begging when you are praying. Instead, start thanking Him because if He has already said it in His word, it already belongs to you. Why are you asking for something that has already been given to you? Your prayer life has to change from begging Him to thanking Him because faith has already said, "Yes." Faith moves. It is tangible. It is a tangible spiritual force. Hebrews 11: 1 says, *Now faith is the substance of things hoped for, the evidence of things not seen.* If it is not now, it is not faith. Faith is laying hold of the unrealities and bringing them into the reality, by acting on the Word of God. So there it goes. Back to that Word, back to the Bible. It is always going to point back to the Word. It is essential that you set yourself in a place where you are not just feeding your spirit on Sunday and Wednesday. As a matter of fact, it is important to feed yourself spiritually on a daily basis. The way technology has developed, you can listen to the Word while you drive to work instead of talking on the phone. You can study the Word online instead of face booking or tweeting. You can eat the Word constantly.

## It Takes Discipline to Eat Right

It is vital that you are listening and feeding yourself something that is actually biblical and not a theory. You can read books, but are you reading about a man's idea, or are you reading from *The Book*? Don't get me wrong, I believe God inspires through writing. I have written some books; you are reading one of them. But everything we hear and everything we read needs to be based on the Word of God. Some books might sound good and make you feel good, but you might not necessarily need to feel good. You might need correction in your life. "Well, I want somebody to uplift me." Well, with faith, correction can uplift you. You do not want to subject yourself to the other side and weigh yourself down with religion and legalism. It is important that you constantly get the Word of God in your spirit.

We are starving ourselves spiritually and wondering why we do not have the strength to win a battle. Remember, the best defense is a good offense. A good offense is staying grounded in the Word of God. The problem is that we have developed a sensational culture that only does what is convenient. God has called us to be disciples. The word disciple comes from the word *discipline*. A disciple is a person who is disciplined. Jesus said, *Take my yoke upon you… my yoke is easy and my burden is light* (Matthew 11:29-30). The word *yoke* translates out to a rabbi's teaching. He says, "Take my teaching upon you and learn of it." Discipline yourself. Deliverance will get you out, but discipline will keep you out. When drama, guilt, worry, fear, doubt, or anything opposite of faith attacks you, you will begin to respond to the enemy like Jesus responded to him in the desert. *Man shall not live by bread alone, but every word that proceeds out of the mouth God* (Matthew 4:4). Get in shape spiritually by having the discipline to eat the Word constantly.

## Building Faith Muscles

Faith is tangible; it is moving. Your faith should never be allowed to stand still because faith will never remain static. It will either strengthen or weaken. It will never stay the same. It is like a level or weight. It goes up or down. The more you feed it, the more it will grow; the less you feed it, the weaker it gets. It is like a muscle that never works out and gets weaker or a muscle that works out and gets stronger. You have to feed it and build it, or it will decline and dissipate. We have to put the pedal to the metal. We have to floor it wide open. We do not have time to let our faith get weak. God has too many big things in store for us.

"Well, I'm in my fifties." It doesn't matter. Smith Wigglesworth was in his sixties when God raised him up. He had an interesting ministry. He would throw you up against a wall, and cancer would fall off you. He would literally pick you up and throw you against a wall. John G. Lake, a man in South Africa, punched a man in the stomach, and there are pictures of him with lightning bolts coming out of his hands and going into the man's body, completely healing him. God is calling us to a higher level of faith. I'm not talking about getting flaky, weird, or psycho. Our faith has to go to a level for the world to see that they do not have to be sick or broke as a joke on a rope. There is a higher way, and that higher way is the Lord Jesus Christ, who is our Savior and Redeemer. He is the King of Kings and Lord of Lords.

111

# CHAPTER 10

## Faith to Possess the Land:
## The Word of Faith

Hebrews 11:1-3 declares:

Now faith is the substance of things hoped for, the evidence of things not seen. For by it *[faith]* the elders obtained a good report. Through faith we understand that the worlds were framed [created] by the word of God, so that things which are seen were not made of things which do appear.

Romans 10:8 adds:

But what saith it? The word is nigh thee, even in thy mouth, and in thy heart: that is, the word of faith, which we preach.

Mark 11:23 proclaims:

For verily I say unto you, That whosoever shall say unto this mountain, Be thou removed, and be thou cast into the sea; and shall not doubt in his heart, but shall believe that those things which he saith shall come to pass; he shall have whatsoever he saith. (KJV)

These Scriptures describe exactly how God began to frame the world and put things into motion in this place we call Earth. We know that God begins to speak by faith, and as He speaks by faith, the world is being framed together. We understand that when we talk about the Word of faith, we are talking about the words that are coming or proceeding out of the mouth of a believer.

We also understand that God has created us in His own image. Therefore, the way God operates is also how He designed believers to operate in this earth to fulfill their purpose and calling. We read in Genesis 1:2 that the spirit of God hovered over the earth and saw it was void and empty. In the next verse, He said, "Let there be light," and there was light. As He speaks it, it begins to manifest. He speaks to the land and the water and causes the waters to divide, and as they divide, the dry ground begins to rise up. He speaks it out of His mouth in faith before seeing anything visible to the natural eye. He speaks it before He sees it with the natural eye.

## Feelings are Liars

You cannot go by your feelings. It is not about what you see; it is not about what you hear; it is not about what you feel. Feelings will lie to you every time. Feelings will tell you that you are not in love. Feelings will tell you that you did not receive your healing. Feelings will tell you all kinds of crazy stuff. They will tell you there is a problem when there is no problem. That is why I tell people that you cannot go by your feelings in your marriage. You cannot go by your feelings in your church. You cannot go by your feelings in anything in your life.

Sometimes you do not have the option to go by your feelings. For example, you do not always feel like getting up and going to work in the morning, but you don't stay home because of your feelings, do you? If you don't go to work, you can't pay the bills and take care of your responsibilities. If you are not led in your feelings about going to work, then do not be led in your feelings concerning relationships, what you have or don't have, where you attend church, or what is going

114

on in your life. Do not invest too much in your feelings. Invest in what God says about your life. Believe that He is not a man that He should lie. If God said He is going to do it, He is going to do it. There is no devil that can stop the hand of God from progressing or moving in your life. Likewise, no person can stop God from manifesting in your life. You have to speak it long enough and consistently enough that the words coming out of your mouth start coming out of your spirit and begin to manifest in the natural.

## Hung by Your Tongue

Jesus performed miracles by his words. We have to get a grip on our words. It is important that you do not allow yourself to speak negatively about your situation. Do not speak negatively about what you are going through, what is happening in your relationships and your family, or even what is happening in your nation. Many people are getting hung by their own tongues because; they receive exactly what they are speaking out of their mouths. When you begin to connect your words to what you are experiencing in your life, you will look back and say, "I said I was going to get that, and I got exactly what I said." Remember, when it comes to Job, they blame everything on the devil. Well, the devil was attacking him, but it really didn't have anything to do with the devil. It was the words that Job was speaking out of his mouth. Go back and read Job. He was speaking negatively.

That is why we should constantly be speaking the blessings of God over our life, our family, our church family, and every person connected to the body of believers. Because when you are blessed, everybody else will be blessed. But we have to start speaking it if we want to see it. We have to start speaking that God's glory is going to manifest to such a degree that before, people will be healed of incurable diseases. We have to start speaking that people are going to fall out under the power of God, and they are going to be filled with the Holy Ghost with the evidence of speaking in other tongues. We have to get a grip on the words we speak out of our mouths. Don't be hung by your own tongue!

## I Will Do It Myself

Allow me to get into a little bit of doctrine. John 12:46-50 states:

For I have not spoken of myself; but the Father which sent me, he gave me a commandment, what I should say, and what I should speak. And I know that his commandment is life everlasting: whatsoever I speak therefore, even as the Father said unto me, so I speak.

Wait a minute. When I speak the word, it is attached to life, not only life but everlasting life. When I speak what God declares, not what I declare, that is when I tap into everlasting life. When we look at this Scripture, Jesus is not talking about a separate individual giving Him instruction. This is actually God's divinity, speaking to God's humane side. Remember, God is in a body suit. In John 14:9, Jesus said, ...*He that hath seen Me hath seen the Father; so how can you say, 'Show us the Father'?* Jesus and the Father are one. Jesus continues in the next verse, ...*The words that I speak to you I do not speak on My own authority; but the Father who dwells in Me...* He is the divinity of God speaking. He is the omnipresent of God speaking. He is the greatness of God speaking. The spiritual side speaks to the natural side through God in the flesh. Remember, Jesus was one hundred percent God and one hundred percent man. He is talking about the communication of the spirit, but He is speaking in a way to help those who come from a specific religion to understand what he is saying. He is speaking of Himself. He says, "When I am speaking of the divinity of God, I am speaking life everlasting."

116

Deuteronomy 18:18 says, *I will raise them up a Prophet from among their brethren, like unto thee, and will put my words in his mouth; and he shall speak unto them all that I shall command him.* You know who the prophet was, right? Jesus. God vacated heaven, put on a body suit, walked the earth, and fulfilled a covenant that no man on earth could fulfill because there was no other man on earth that was without sin. God tried with Abraham. He tried with Moses. He tried going all the way through the Old Covenant, but none of them had the ability to fulfill it. So He said, "I will go down and do it myself. I will finish it once and for all."

## Faith in Your Faith

Matthew 12:37 states, *For by thy words thou shalt be justified, and by thy words thou shalt be condemned.* Why do I stay on this subject? I want you to get it. I want you to stop speaking death over your life, family, and relationships and start speaking life into it. That is what motivated me to write this chapter, the Word of Faith. Proverbs 18:4 says, *The words of a man's mouth are as deep waters, and the wellspring of wisdom as a flowing brook.* The Books of Genesis to Revelation constantly reiterates the doctrine of your words and the importance of getting a grip on them. You have to declare your needs by faith even though you cannot see the results in the natural.

You have to have faith in your faith. It doesn't matter if you speak it if you do not believe the very thing you speak. So you have to be willing to believe your own words. Let me ask you something. When you say, "Oh, God's going to bless me," do you really believe it? Do you truly believe that He is going to bless you? Do you really believe that God is going to make you a millionaire, or are you just saying it because everyone else in the room is saying it? Do you have faith in your faith? Do you believe that God is not a man that he should lie? Do you believe that if He said He would do it in your life, He would do it? When we begin to have faith in our faith, believing our words and nothing else, God will perform it.

You have to stop believing you are too unworthy to have faith. You must stop believing you are unfit for what God has called you to do. The only way you will start having faith in your faith and believing your words is to stop believing the words of the enemy. Stop believing the words of your abusive father or whoever has talked down to you in your life. You must stop believing the negative and start believing what heaven has already declared over your life. He has declared that you are the head and not the tail, above and not beneath, blessed in the city, blessed in the field, blessed going in, blessed going out, and everything you put your hands to is blessed.

Remember, blessed is past tense. It is already there. You have already been blessed, healed, and raised up. You just have to believe that when you speak it, God will bring it to pass in your life. As a matter of fact, some of you should just shake off the attitude, unworthiness, unfitness, fear, and weakness. They told you that you don't have enough faith. Oh no, He has already given you a measure of faith. You have all the faith you need. You have to shake off all the lies of the enemy because you are who God says you are. You are a child of the King of Kings and the Lord of Lords.

## Words of Faith

Someone reading this chapter is about to get the most significant breakthrough of their life. You have that one thing holding on to you, but I declare right now that the Lord has already crushed the head of the enemy in your life. You are not going back. You are not going to suffer. You are not going to be bound any longer. The chains have been broken. Give Him praise. He is delivering you right now. Just shout,

"The chains are falling off. My days of being broke are over. My days of being depressed are over. I will not be depressed, oppressed, or possessed any longer. He who the Son sets free is free indeed, and the King of Kings and the Lord of Lords is on my side. If God is for me, who can be against me? The enemy will come in one way, but he will flee seven different ways because my God will use him as a footstool. And here I am; they might have counted me out, but I am still standing because I still have some faith left inside me."

Is anybody reading this grateful for the blood that was shed at Calvary? If it had not been for the blood, you would have been dead a long time ago. Because of the blood, you can approach the throne of grace boldly. Because of the blood, you can lift your hands, open your mouth, and say, "Yes, I am qualified. Yes, I am worthy because of what Jesus did on the cross." Out of the abundance of the heart the mouth will speak. You have to get that junk out of your trunk. Clean it out right now. You have to get that wrong belief system out. You have to get that wrong talking out. Get it out and let your faith-filled words dominate. Faith-filled words will always dominate over the law of death.

## Words of Resurrection Power

John 11:38-44 gives the account of Jesus raising Lazarus from the dead:

Jesus therefore again groaning in himself cometh to the grave. It was a cave, and a stone lay upon it. Jesus said, Take ye away the stone. Martha, the sister of him that was dead, saith unto him, Lord, by this time he stinketh: for he hath been dead four days. Jesus saith unto her, Said I not unto thee, that, if thou wouldest believe, thou shouldest see the glory of God? Then they took away the stone from the place where the dead was laid. And Jesus lifted up his eyes, and said, Father, I thank thee that thou hast heard me. And I knew that thou hearest me always: but because of the people which stand by I said it, that they may believe that thou hast sent me. And when he thus had spoken, he cried with a loud voice, Lazarus, come forth. And he that was dead came forth, bound hand and foot with graveclothes: and his face was bound about with a napkin. Jesus saith unto them, Loose him, and let him go. (KJV)

In the New Testament, as Jesus begins to operate in his ministry, He raised the dead, healed the sick, stilled the sea, and He did it all with His words. You will never see Jesus operate any other way in His ministry. He always spoke it out of his mouth before it manifested into the atmosphere. In Luke 17:19, He said, *Your faith has made you whole.* In John 5:11 and 12, He said, *Rise up and be healed, pick up your bed and walk.* He speaks into a tomb with a dead man wrapped up in grave clothes and says, "Lazarus, it doesn't matter if you have been dead four days; when I speak, I am going to cause life to come back into your bones. I am going to cause life to come back into your heart. Your heart is going to beat again. Your blood is going to develop new cells again. Because when I speak, all heaven stands at attention, and the earth stands still. The blessings of God begin to manifest out of my spirit and into the atmosphere."

When Jesus spoke to His friend, Lazarus, he had been dead for four days, but Jesus still said, "Roll away the stone." Everyone said, "But he's been dead four days." But Jesus said, "It doesn't matter how long. Did I not tell you that I am the resurrection of life? All authority has been given unto me." So, they rolled the stone back, and the stench began to fill the air. When God is about to do something big, He always brings critics to watch. The Pharisees and Sadducees could not see it. They were sitting watching and covering their nose because the smell was so bad. Have you ever felt like you were dead when you walked into a room just by the expression people give you or the lack of quality in their conversation? Have you ever felt like the world had rolled a stone over you and considered you done because you made too many mistakes or committed too many sins? You love the Lord, but you have that one thing that always holds you back. You know it, and they know it. It is almost like you spilled something on your shirt, and everybody can see it.

Everyone was asking, "What is Jesus doing? It has been four days; He is all tied up in grave clothes." What you have to understand is that a tomb actually went down into the ground. Lazarus is tied up and down several feet in the ground. Even if he is alive, he does not have the ability to get out of the ground because he is bound. He can't walk up the stairs and out of the tomb. Jesus said, "I have come so that God may get the glory." Don't ever belittle what you have been through in your life because God will get glory out of it all. Even with your mistakes, He loves you so much; He will get the glory out of it. God can still use you. He can still work through you.

So he begins to speak. Have you ever wondered why He called his name? He commands, "Lazarus, come forth." He had to speak his name because if he didn't, He would resurrect the whole graveyard. That is why you need to get more specific with your words when you are believing God for something. He speaks, "Lazarus come forth," and a stinky body tied up and rotting is elevated out of the tomb. When God brings you back to life, He doesn't leave you where you are lying. He picks you up to elevate you where He has called you. Jesus brings him to the top, and people begin to run frantically. There stood a man who was dead four days ago. He escaped death because another man spoke words of resurrection power out of His mouth. Those words dominated the natural laws of this world.

I believe we are entering into a season of seeing creative miracles. We have to start speaking the same thing as a body of believers. We can pray for revival, but nothing will happen until we all speak the same thing in unity. Let it be like an echo that travels across the land that something miraculous is happening in our nation. And let those words bring life to everything that is dead. Let the words of resurrection power say, "You shall live again." Jesus did nothing for himself; He did everything for you and me, and because of what He did for us, we are kingdom heirs to receive everything that is His.

Ephesians 2:4-6 states:

But God, who is rich in mercy, for his great love wherewith he loved us, Even when we were dead in sins, hath quickened us together with Christ, (by grace ye are saved;) And hath raised us up together, and made us sit together in heavenly places in Christ Jesus: (KJV)

You must get back up no matter how badly you have messed up. God said, "You were dead, but I resurrected you with my words, with the word of faith, and now it is time for you to take your seat in Christ." When you begin to take your place and assume your rights and privileges, God is going to respond to you. "I receive everything you have for my life. I receive purpose. I receive destiny. I receive it by the Holy Ghost. I call those things not as though they were. I am not going to be the victim anymore. I am going to be the victor, and I am going to confess and speak your blessings over my life, over my health, over my marriage, and over my family. We don't need to talk it out. We just need to speak it out, and God will perform it. His Word confirms it. If you can speak the results you want, He will bring it to pass. Speak the Word of faith.

# Faith That Conquers Fear

## Part III

# CHAPTER 11

## Faith That Conquers Fear:
## Walking in Constant Faith

What does it mean to walk in constant faith? 1 Timothy 6:12 exclaims, *Fight the good fight of faith, lay hold on eternal life, whereunto thou art also called, and hast professed a good profession before many witnesses.* (KJV)

Colossians 1:23 proclaims:

*[And this He will do]* provided that you continue to stay with and in the faith *[in Christ]*, well-grounded and settled and steadfast, not shifting or moving away from the hope *[which rests on and is inspired by]* the glad tidings (the Gospel), which you heard and which has been preached *[as being designed for and offered without restrictions]* to every person under heaven, and of which *[Gospel]* I, Paul, became a minister. (AMPC)

*And this He will do,* provided we continue to stay with and in the faith. Everything God does in our life is contingent upon us constantly walking in the realm of faith. *If you continue to stay with and in faith in Christ, well-grounded, settled, and steadfast,* He will perform it. But, you cannot be well grounded if your roots are not in the ground. If you are a potted plant, and I am not talking about the stuff you toke, you can be moved around. But when you have been planted in the ground, and your roots begin to expand, it will take a lot to pull you out of the ground. ...*Well-grounded and settled and steadfast, not shifting or moving away from the hope* [which rests on and is inspired by] *the glad tidings (the Gospel), which you heard and which has been preached* [as being designed for and offered without restrictions] *to every person under heaven, and of which* [Gospel] *I, Paul, became a minister.* There are no restrictions to the measure of faith God wants to give you.

You do not really know what is happening in the world until you get out of America and actually see what is taking place in other countries. One of the things I have noticed while traveling in eighteen nations of the world is that many people are having a problem walking in faith because of several common issues. They are hindered by the carnality of their minds. The enemy is constantly throwing in front of them and reminding them of their past mistakes, things they have done, or things that happened to them in the past. To overcome this mentality, they have to understand what Jesus did for them when He went to the cross. We have to get a revelation on how He freed us in order before we can walk in the fullness of what He has for our life.

## A New Thing

If it were about you saving yourself from sin, you would have done it long ago. And if you could save yourself from sin, there would be no reason for Jesus to go to the cross at Calvary. Everything is in Him and by Him. You can't save yourself. You can't dress well enough. You can't talk good enough. You can't say the right things. You can't do anything in your own effort to save yourself and eternally secure yourself. Everything that has been done in your life concerning your salvation, faith, and walk with God has everything to do with what He has done and nothing to do with your good behavior.

As a matter of fact, your good behavior is only a result of what He has done for you. Did you catch that? Your righteousness is a result of what Christ has accomplished at Calvary. Many people do not have an understanding or have a revelation on what it actually means to be a new creation or a new creature in Christ. 2 Corinthians 5:17 says, *Therefore, if anyone is in Christ, the new creation has come: The old has gone, the new is here* (NIV). Now this is not only talking about what you did before you confessed Christ or were baptized. It is also talking about what you did yesterday, two minutes ago, or thirty seconds ago. It is talking about every second that passes in time. You have to understand that you have been made new. You are a new creation in Christ, and the old things, the old ways, the old behaviors, and the old actions are passed away, and God is doing a new thing in you now!

When we go by our senses, we think what we see does not align with what He is saying. But that is why we have to understand that we never go by our five senses. We go by faith; we still speak, "I am the righteousness of God. I am the righteousness of Christ Jesus. The old things have passed away. All things are being made new. They are made new and are being made new, and I am not the person I used to be. That person is no longer me that liveth, but Christ that liveth within me. I have been crucified with Christ." We must understand that the old man is being crucified at the cross with Christ, and we have been raised up as a new creature for such a time as this. Say right now, "I am not what I used to do. I am not who I used to be. I am free because who the Son sets free, He is free indeed."

## God's Eyes Only

Colossians 1:21-23 explain it like this:

Once you were alienated from God and were enemies in your minds because of your evil behavior. But now he has reconciled you by Christ's physical body through death to present you holy in his sight, without blemish and free from accusation— if you continue in your faith, established and firm, and do not move from the hope held out in the gospel. This is the gospel that you heard and that has been proclaimed to every creature under heaven, and of which I, Paul, have become a servant. (NIV)

In God's eyes, you have already been reconciled because of what has been accomplished at Calvary. He made you a new creature. Anytime He sees you, He sees His blood on you. He sees you through the blood of Christ. He sees you holy. He sees you whole. He sees you renewed. He is not looking at a jacked-up person. He looks at a person healed, restored, and renewed because God doesn't look by the flesh. He only looks by faith. When everyone else looks at all the wrongs you have done, God says, "I do not look at the wrong you have done; I look at the right I have done within you." Naysayers will say, "No, you will never amount to anything," but they cannot compete with God saying, "Yes, you will amount to everything that I called you to be." God sees us through His eyes only.

## More Than a Conqueror

According to 1 Peter 1:5, we have been reborn: *Who are kept by the power of God through faith unto salvation ready to be revealed in the last time.* There's that *faith* word again, that f-word. Some of you need to learn how to drop the f-bomb. Start talking the f-word. Someone is about to get a revelation. You are born again; it is the power of God through faith into salvation. Reborn means that you have been revealed as a new creation in Christ Jesus. Again, why do people keep sinning? Because they believe they are sinners. It has nothing to do with their dress, makeup, haircut, or anything else. It is because they believe they are sinners. You have to stop believing that you are a sinner and start believing that you are the head and not the tail, you are above and not beneath, you are the righteousness of God in Christ Jesus, and you are an heir of the king. The old man, the old nature, and the old carnality will die, and something new will begin. The new creation reality will begin to rise up on the inside of you.

Let's go a little deeper with this. Revelation 1:4-6 reveals:

John to the seven churches which are in Asia: Grace be unto you, and peace, from him which is, and which was, and which is to come; and from the seven Spirits which are before his throne; And from Jesus Christ, who is the faithful witness, and the first begotten of the dead, and the prince of the kings of the earth. Unto him that loved us, and washed us… And hath made us kings and priests unto God and his Father; to him be glory and dominion for ever and ever. Amen. (KJV)

Verse 5 states, ...*Unto him that loved us, and washed us.* Loved and washed is in the past tense. Quit asking forgiveness for something He has already provided. As a matter of fact, Psalm 103:12 states, *As far as the east is from the west, so far hath he removed our transgressions from us.* You do not have to keep bringing something up that He has already taken care of. Verse 6 continues, *"And hath made us kings and priests."* Why do you still have the mentality of a slave? He has made you a king and a priest unto himself. He is saying, "I made you a king, and I am waiting for you to show up and act like it." Peter 2:9 declares, *But ye are a chosen generation, a royal priesthood, an holy nation, a peculiar people; that ye should shew forth the praises of him who hath called you out of darkness into his marvellous light.* You cannot be a chosen generation, a royal priesthood, and still be a sinner. You have to decide which one you are going to be. You must decide whether you want to be a sinner or a chosen generation and the royal priesthood He has called you to be. And then He says, "Let me go ahead and put something on top of it. You are a holy nation. You are not holy because of what you did. You are holy because of what I did for you at Calvary."

Romans 8:35 says, *Who shall separate us from the love of Christ? shall tribulation, or distress, or persecution, or famine, or nakedness, or peril, or sword?* Not even your sin can separate you from the love of Christ. You are more than a conqueror. Is there anybody reading this who will say, "I am more than a conqueror? I am not who I used to be. I conquered that through the blood which was shed at Calvary. I am in Christ now."

## Getting Your But in the Right Place

Ephesians 2:10-13 declares:

For we are his workmanship, created in Christ Jesus unto good works, which God hath before ordained that we should walk in them. Wherefore remember, that ye being in time past Gentiles in the flesh, who are called Uncircumcision by that which is called the Circumcision in the flesh made by hands; That at that time ye were without Christ, being aliens from the commonwealth of Israel, and strangers from the covenants of promise, having no hope, and without God in the world: But now in Christ Jesus ye who sometimes were far off are made nigh by the blood of Christ. (KJV)

Back up a minute. Did you know we have so much legalism and religion in the church that if some had their way, they would still be circumcising people today, attempting to make them more holy? This Scripture explains that it is not by the circumcision of the hands. Your flesh is never going to get the job done. You can put a wig on a dead body. You can put sleeves down to the wrist. But at the end of the day, it is still a dead body. It will not get done if Christ doesn't do it in you. You can still be jacked up, messed up, and still lost in the world, but if Christ does it in you, no man can stop the work of the Lord from manifesting in your life.

130

Verse 13 says, *But now in Christ Jesus ye who sometimes were far off are made nigh by the blood of Christ.* Get your but in the right place. *But* now, you are made nigh by the what? Are you made nigh by your good behavior or the way you dress? No. Are you made nigh because you don't have a beard, you don't wear makeup, your grandma went to church, or you have attended the same church for so long? No to all the above. You are made nigh by the what? *But* now you are made nigh by the blood of Christ.

## Unlearning Learned Doctrine

Ephesians 1:13 declares, *In whom ye also trusted, after that ye heard the word of truth, the gospel of your salvation: in whom also after that ye believed, ye were sealed with that holy Spirit of promise,* You were sealed with the Holy Ghost when you received the Holy Ghost. He ensured you were airtight so the old man could never get in again. You are sealed. It is a done deal. Do not let the devil lie and tell you that you have messed up too much.

Go back to Colossians 1:12-14

Giving thanks unto the Father, which hath made us meet to be partakers of the inheritance of the saints in light: Who hath delivered us from the power of darkness, and hath translated us into the kingdom of his dear Son: In whom we have redemption through his blood, even the forgiveness of sins: (KJV)

There is an inheritance for the believer. *Had delivered us* is also in the past tense. Quit trying to get delivered when you have already been delivered. The only thing that needs to shift is your belief system. He moved you out of sin and placed you as king in the priesthood. He translated you. He instantly moved you from one place to another.

Somebody will ask, "What about sanctification?" It is not that God needs to be sanctified. It is your mind that needs to be converted to believe what has already been done. It is all in the mind. I was talking to my wife one night. We were talking about doctrine on different subjects. It gets interesting when you start talking about doctrine. To unlearn the learned doctrine that is instilled in a person's life doesn't take days, weeks, or months. It takes years. As a matter of fact, it takes ten years for people to really start grasping the revelation of faith. It takes that long for the light to finally click on for people to start operating in faith. It doesn't take God that long; it takes us that long to undo all the wrong so we can get in all the right. It is amazing how religion complicates it. It is not the unsaved that give Pastors most of the problems; it is the religious people. Unsaved people are also indoctrinated with religious tradition either through their family members or by attending religious church services. Self-righteous doctrine must be rooted out of our thinking in order to operate in constant faith. We have to unlearn all of our learned religion by renewing our minds with the Word of God.

## Redeemed From What?

We have redemption, right? Revelation 5:9 says, *And they sung a new song, saying, Thou art worthy to take the book, and to open the seals thereof: for thou wast slain, and hast redeemed us to God by thy blood out of every kindred, and tongue, and people, and nation;* When you are saved and redeemed, you are not going to sing that old tune you have always been singing. Let me put it this way. When you get a revelation of who you are in Christ, you won't say the things you used to say. And when you don't say the things you used to say, you'll start saying things by faith. And when you start speaking things by faith, you'll start walking in constant faith.

132

What have you been redeemed from? Romans 6:10 says: *For in that he died, he died unto sin once: but in that he liveth, he liveth unto God...* So you have been redeemed from spiritual death. What does that mean? John 3:5 says that if a man be born again, he must be born again of water and spirit. So when he is born of water and spirit, he has been redeemed from spiritual death; therefore, his spirit can no longer die. You cannot kill a man who is full of the Holy Ghost. We all know the flesh days are numbered, but the spirit lives forever. We have also been redeemed from sickness and disease. Romans 8:2 confirms, *For the law of the spirit of life in Christ Jesus has made us free from the law of sin and death.* When we operate in that constant faith, knowing who we are in Christ, we exercise our authority and power through Christ to overcome sickness, death, and disease.

We have the power. Never operate under fear. Faith and fear cannot operate in the same body. To constantly walk in faith, you cannot let up one second, especially when you are fighting for something. If the devil can get in your thoughts, he will talk you into taking your foot off the accelerator. If you give him an inch, he will take a mile. You have to press in. You have to push hard. You have to believe. If we are ever going to see our cities shaken by the mighty hand of God, we cannot have some mediocre service or a good one here and a bad one there. No, we have to go to church hungry every time. We have to go thirsty every time. We have to go with a shout of praise in our hearts every time we walk in the doors. We must walk in with our faith at an all-time high because souls are hanging in the balance of eternity, and we cannot afford to take our foot off the accelerator.

He has also redeemed you from poverty. Broke folk can't do anything for the kingdom. Broke folk can't do anything because Broke needs a ride. Broke hangs out after church waiting for someone to invite them to eat because they can't afford to go out alone. When you are blessed, you can take everybody out to eat. Galatians 3:13 proclaims, *For*

*Christ has redeemed us from the curse of the law and being made a curse for us for it is written cursed is every man that hangeth on a tree.* He said that He took the curse on himself so that it can never hang over your head again. It was nailed to the cross. As you read and receive this, you have to make the decision that you are going to walk in constant faith.

## To God Be the Glory

Faith only operates in love. Hebrews 10:38 *Now the just shall live by faith: but if any man draw back, my soul shall have no pleasure in him.* A drawback could be any hatred, ought, offense, insecurity, or anything drawing you back from expressing the love of Christ. Can you love them when they spit in your face? Can you love them when they talk badly about you behind your back? Okay, you said, "I forgive them, but I do not have to be around them?" Can you love them enough to forgive them and be in the same room with them? Can you put your nose down and let them know that it doesn't matter what they said or did; the ground is level at the cross? Can you love them even when they don't love you? Can you say, "I am going to be the one who puts the oil or the wine on the wounds? I am going to pick you up and put you on my donkey. I am going to pay for your place to stay because God is not finished with you, just like he wasn't finished with me."

Romans 3:27 says, *Where is boasting then? It is excluded. By what law? of works? Nay: but by the law of faith.* This Scripture is saying that you should put your nose down and just chill out. Quit acting like you have it all together on your own. It is all by the law of faith in Christ Jesus, who is the one true Living God. It is by Him, through Him, and in Him that you and I operate in life. Every time God does something in our life, is why we always say, "To God be the glory." Because the minute you take credit for it, you will also take the criticism. I don't want the criticism, so I give Him all the credit.

## The Name

The result of constantly walking by faith is fearlessly using the name of Jesus. Some of us just casually say it; we don't really have faith in our faith and believe in the name. But when you get a revelation on the power of that name, you will speak it out in faith without fear. You will know that all heaven and hell stands at attention when you speak that name. You will know that it is by that name men are saved, devils are cast out, the blind see, and the dead are raised. It is by the name of Jesus that men are baptized, and their sins are washed away. It is by that name that every knee should bow, and every tongue shall confess that Jesus Christ is Lord. It is the name above every other name, the name of Jesus Christ. And it is faith in that name that will produce what you need.

1 John 3:23 says:

And this is his commandment, That we should believe on the name of his Son Jesus Christ, and love one another, as he gave us commandment. And his name through faith in his name hath made this man strong, whom ye see and know: yea, the faith which is by him hath given him this perfect soundness in the presence of you all. (KJV)

2 Peter 1:1 says, *Simon Peter, a servant and an apostle of Jesus Christ, to them that have obtained like precious faith with us through the righteousness of God and our Saviour Jesus Christ:* It is through Christ and His name that we obtain everything from heaven, every inheritance, and everything for which we are believing. I have to ask you, "Do you still believe in the name? Do you still believe that it is by that name that men are saved? Are you in a "name believing" church that believes that it is by that name men are saved?" It is by that name that revival comes. It is by that name that your city will be turned upside down for the glory of God. It is by that name - the name of Jesus.

135

# Prophecy

No more will you be bound by your past. And no more will you rehearse what has been said or done to you; it has all been put away from you as far as the East is from the West. You will rise up in the name of Christ Jesus and confess that you are no longer bound by addiction. You are no longer bound by bad relationships. I am going to go ahead and confess that you are no longer bound by soul ties, either. You are no longer bound by the opinions of people from your past. How they saw you in your past does not define who you are today.

I prophesy that you are a new creation in Christ. Rise up and walk in faith knowing that your God has gone before you and made the crooked path straight. Lift your hands. You didn't mess up too terribly. You cannot go too low. Religion is telling you that lie. There is no place too low that His hand can't reach you. He says, "If you will reach up, I will reach out and pull you up. For, I made you a chosen generation. You did not choose me, but I chose you."

# CHAPTER 12

*Faith That Conquers Fear:*
## Having Faith in Your Faith

You have faith, but do you have faith in your faith?

Hebrews 12:1-2 declares:

Wherefore seeing we also are compassed about with so great a cloud of witnesses, let us lay aside every weight, and the sin which doth so easily beset us, and let us run with patience the race that is set before us, Looking unto Jesus the author and finisher of our faith; who for the joy that was set before him endured the cross, despising the shame, and is set down at the right hand of the throne of God. (KJV)

1 John 1-5 declares:

Whosoever believeth that Jesus is the Christ is born of God: and every one that loveth him that begat loveth him also that is begotten of him. By this we know that we love the children of God, when we love God, and keep his commandments. For this is the love of God, that we keep his commandments: and his commandments are not grievous. For whatsoever is born of God overcometh the world: and this is the victory that overcometh the world, even our faith. Who is he that overcometh the world, but he that believeth that Jesus is the Son of God? (KJV)

As we read Hebrews 12:1-2, we understand that Jesus is the author of our faith. He is the centerpiece of everything, and when you have faith in your faith, it will always point you back to what Christ did for you. I don't know about you, but if it weren't for Jesus on my side, I wouldn't be here because there would not be any air in my lungs. But because of his goodness, mercy, and grace, I am still standing as I write this book, and you are still standing with me as you read it because God has a plan for our life.

## Familiarity Breeds Contempt

A lot of times, we lose respect for what were once our miracles. We become redundant in the things of God and lose that excitement we used to have when someone gets saved or baptized. When we have baptisms at our church, many people leave early. They have become complacent with the understanding that all of Heaven rejoices over one sinner coming to repentance. When we become familiar with the things of God, we lose respect for what He has done in our lives. We also lose respect for what He is doing in other people's lives. We don't understand that familiarity is weakening our faith to receive what God has for our lives.

You can't have faith in your faith if you lose sight of what God has done for you. It is hard to be confident in something if you do not understand that if he did it before, he could do it again. I don't know about you, but I still get excited when I think about how He saved me. I get excited when I think about how He delivered my brother from drugs. Even though it was years ago, I am still excited to be saved, sanctified, and filled with the Holy Ghost.

When God heals somebody, we just say, "Oh, praise the Lord." No, when you understand that the Lord just healed and touched somebody, and you want more of it, you must learn to celebrate what's already been given to you. How can you expect God to save your family when you don't even personally celebrate what He's done in your life? How can you expect God to do the miraculous in people's lives around you if you can't stand up and give God praise and thank him that you have air in your lungs? I don't want to be known as someone who overlooks God's goodness. I want to celebrate the little wins and the big wins. I want to celebrate when somebody gets a new car or a new house. I want to celebrate when somebody gets a twenty-five cent an hour raise. If it weren't for the Lord on my side, the enemy would have already destroyed me. But thank God the enemy missed, and God brought me into a wealthy place. Can you still celebrate Him? Are you still excited that He went to the Cross but didn't stay on the cross; He rose up and defeated death, hell, and the grave?

When are you going to get your shout back? When are you going to get your praise back? You're waiting for God to do it, and he is saying, "I'm waiting for you to open your mouth and praise me." See, my praise is an indication of who my faith is in. My faith is not in my government. My faith is not in my job. My faith is not in my family. My faith is in the King of Kings and the Lord of Lords, Jesus, the only one true Living God. When you get a revelation of it, you don't need music to help you shout. You don't need a cheerleader to help you praise Him. Before the music ever starts, you will be at the altar dancing because you remember where you were. You were about to lose your mind. Lord, help us never to get familiar with your glory. Help us never to get familiar with what you have done for us. Help us never to allow our familiarity to breed contempt for the things of God.

## Why Jesus?

Ask yourself, "What has He done for me?" He was your substitute. Romans 8:32 says, *He who did not spare his own Son, but gave him up*

139

*for us all—how will he not also, along with him, graciously give us all things?* Because of what He has done at Calvary, we have extended grace. We have extended mercy. We have extended healing. We have extended deliverance. He went in our place. It should have been us nailed to that cross. But, He went before us and made the crooked path straight. It was Him all along, and it had nothing to do with us.

He is also your intercessor. Hebrews 7:25 says, *Therefore he is able to save completely those who come to God through him, because he always lives to intercede for them."* Do you understand that He is interceding for you? He is speaking up for you when nobody else will. He is declaring His Word over your life when someone, maybe even a family member, rejected you, talked against you, lied on you, cheated on you, and stole from you. But God says, "No, I still have plans for you. I am still working everything together for the good because you love me, and I have called you for such a time as this." Is there anybody else who is excited that when the world rejects you, labels you dead, puts you in the tomb, and seals it, Jesus shows up on the scene and says, "Roll the stone away; you might think they are dead, but I'm just getting started with them, and I'm going to show the world that what I bless, no man can curse." If you ever begin to get complacent in your relationship with God, just remember what He did for you at Calvary and that He is interceding on your behalf.

## Word Drive-thru

We don't have a faith problem; we have a Word problem. We create dry cleaning services on Sundays where people come for sixty minutes to get a little swish-swish-swish. Or the service is like a drive-thru where people drive in and order three Holy Ghost shakes and a Word-a-burger and drive off. There is no conviction. There is no power. There is no anointing. There is no Word. It is the washing of the Word that converts the soul and brings about the process of sanctification in our life.

We know that when we receive Christ and are born again, we are given a measure of faith. Romans 12:3 states, *For by the grace given me I say to every one of you* [everybody]: *Do not think of yourself more highly than you ought, but rather think of yourself with sober judgment, in accordance with the faith God has distributed to each of you.* You can have something and not know how to work it. You are asking for something God has already given you, but you will never know how to work it until you work the Word. Tweet that. If you work the Word through faith, the Word will work for you.

There is a lack of revelation of the Word because we create drive-thru services, not allowing people to be changed by the power of the Word. The Word of God is the power of God. The Bible says that the gospel is the power unto salvation. If you only get the Word on Sunday morning and Wednesday night, you are already starving yourself. The Word has to be taken in on a daily basis. Technology rules out the excuses because it makes the Word more available to you now than it has ever been in the past. You might have to turn off Netflix. I spend most of my time in the Word in the wee hours of the night when everyone is asleep. You have to submerge yourself. Somebody says, "I'm busy." Everybody is busy, but are you being productive? You have to get the Word in you.

## How Does Faith Come?

As a kid growing up, I'll never forget that my mom would lay me down and pray for me and play the Bible on tape every single night. It would automatically play the other side of the tape, so I would get a full tape of the Word. I would sleep with that Word playing. Somebody said, "Well, what good will that do?" Listen, you don't catch the word with your mind; you catch it with your spirit. Every night I was catching it with my spirit. I was feeding my spirit. I don't say this braggingly, but most of the time, as I prepare a message to preach, I know where every Scripture I seek is. I give my mom credit because listening to those tapes over and over, it got in my spirit. It is just like a word of knowledge or gift of knowledge. You just know it. When you are feeding your spirit, you just know it. When you need it, it is there. When the enemy tempted Jesus, how did he respond? He responded with the Word. When the Word connects with your faith, and you start responding to circumstances by faith through the Word, you begin to activate supernatural power.

How does faith come? Romans 10:17 says, *So then faith cometh by hearing, and hearing by the word of God.* You have to hear the Word for your faith to expand so God can give you that for which you are believing. You need to turn the music off and turn the Word up. As I said before, half of the music we listen to is not biblically sound. I have asked our praise team to take a whole verse out of a song because it was not biblical. Why? Because when you are in the worship service, you receive the Word. That is the whole point. When you are full of the Word, it comes to you by nature. You quote it without realizing it. It comes out of your pores. You respond to everything with the Word. You do not walk by sight; you walk by faith. It will just start getting into your DNA and who you are. But you have to hear the Word before faith comes.

## Who Can Have Faith?

The familiar verses of Mark 11:22-23 explain:

And Jesus answering saith unto them, Have faith in God. For verily I say unto you, That whosoever shall say unto this mountain, Be thou removed, and be thou cast into the sea; and shall not doubt in his heart, but shall believe that those things which he saith shall come to pass; he shall have whatsoever he saith. (KJV)

Faith works for whosoever shall say. Are you a whosoever? If you are a whosoever, you can have faith. We are talking about having faith in your faith. Do you believe when you say, "In the name of Jesus, mountain be thou removed," the mountain actually moves right then, or do you believe that it is going to move later? Hebrews 11:1 says, *Now faith is the substance of things hoped for, the evidence of things not seen.* If it is not now, it is not faith. When do you believe the mountain is removed and cast into the sea? You believe the minute you speak it out of your mouth. When you believe He does it at that moment, you will stop begging for things that you desire in your life. To have faith, you must have faith that God does it right then.

John 5:5 says, *Who is he that overcometh the world, but he that believeth that Jesus is the Son of God?* It is faith that overcomes. It is your faith, having faith in your faith. Who is he that overcomes the world? He that believes that Jesus is the Son of God overcomes the world. So you are putting your faith in Christ. But you have to believe that what you say is actually going to happen. To have faith, you have to have faith in what you say.

Let's talk about the great exchanger. 1 Thessalonians 5:10 says, *Who died for us, that, whether we wake or sleep, we should live together with him.* So there's an exchange here. Galatians 2:20 says, *I am crucified with Christ: nevertheless I live; yet not I, but Christ liveth in me: and the life which I now live in the flesh I live by the faith* [the f-bomb again] *of the Son of God, who loved me, and gave himself for me.* He became poor so that you might be rich. He became sin so that you might be saved. You have to have faith in that. You must have faith in what was accomplished at Calvary to have faith.

143

II Corinthians 5:21 says, *For he hath made him to be sin for us, who knew no sin; that we might be made the righteousness of God in him.* Why are you still calling yourself a sinner? Why do you still possess the consciousness of a sinner when He became sin so that you could be righteous? You are in sin because you still have a sin mentality. You will stop sinning when you start believing in what He has done for your life. He made you righteous, didn't He? That is what the Book says. He became weak so that we could be strong. He suffered shame to give us glory. How about this, He went to hell so you can go to heaven. Thank God, He didn't stay there. He defeated death, hell, and the grave. He was condemned to set us free. To have faith, you have to have faith that you are righteous in Him.

## Battle of the Mind

Our struggle is not with God. You have to get a revelation of this, or you will never activate your faith. Your struggle is not with the Lord. Your struggle is with your mentality. It is with your mindset. Your struggle is that you do not have faith in your faith. You do not have faith in what He has done; therefore, you are constantly second-guessing yourself. You know you slipped up the night before, so when you say, "In the name of Jesus," you question whether it worked or not. Then you blame it on the devil. Listen, it had nothing to do with the devil. I think sometimes the devil stands before the Lord and says, "Look, I'm sorry; I didn't really do it that time. It was all them; I promise you." I have met people I wanted to lay hands on and say, "Come out of that devil in the name of Jesus." We, as Pentecostals, are classic about blaming others, or the enemy, to justify what we do, and it has nothing to do with him. It is just that you do not have a revelation yet. The veil is still over your eyes. We have to stop justifying the way we are and just say, "Lord, I have to change my carnality."

144

## Revelation Knowledge

How do you get a revelation of the Word? Get a revelation of Jesus. In Matthew 16:13-18, Jesus asked the disciples, "Who do men say that I am?" They said, "Some say you are a prophet. Some say you are John the Baptist. Others say you are the Prophet, Elijah," but then He turned to them and said, "But who do you say I am? Peter stands up and says, "I believe you are the Christ, Son of the Living God." Jesus said, "Blessed are you, Peter, for flesh and blood did not reveal this to you. The divinity of who I am has revealed this to you." He goes on to say, "Upon this rock I will build my church, and the gates of hell shall not prevail against it." Another word for rock is revelation. He said, "I will build my church upon the revelation of who I really am."

God will start to build your life when you get a revelation of who He really is. God is saying that when you get the revelation of who He is, He will build you up, and the gates of hell shall not prevail against you. Somebody reading this is getting a revelation right now. You will not have to worry about the devil one more day in your life. It wasn't the rocks that took out Goliath; it was the revelation. He said, "I come in the name of the Lord." Do you have faith in the name that is above every name that every knee shall bow and every tongue shall confess... the name by which men are saved? Do you have a revelation of the name?

## Shout Doubt Out

You have to stop believing anything that is the opposite of what God has already done. You have to exercise your faith. Doubt will not leave voluntarily. It must be kicked out. You have to kick doubt out with your praise. Doubt is not going to leave by just asking it to. You need to evict that thing out of your house. Shout, "Doubt out." Say,

"Get out of my house. Get out of my money. Get out of my finances and get out of my children's life. Get out. Get out. Get out of my family. Get out of my house and get out of my job. There is no place here for you any longer. There is no place for you to stay. Doubt, you must get out because He has already spoken it, and if God has already spoken it, baby, you can take it to the bank because it is a done deal." Kick it out. Kick it out of your job. Kick it out of your promotion and kick it out of your children. Kick the doubt out because God's coming in. You must kick it out of your mind. You have to kick it out of your heart. You have to kick it out of your marriage, and you have to kick it out of your family. Kick it out. Shout doubt out!

## Snake Eggs

You have to kick the snake out. Let me tell you what happens if you do not kick it out. Doubt is a snake; if you don't kick it out, it will lay eggs in your head (mind) and have snakes growing in that space. And do you know what comes with doubt? The answer is fear. It could be that something is growing in your head because you didn't kick it out in time. Oh, but I am ready. I have my kicking shoes on. I cast that devil out in the mighty name of Jesus. I cast out fear. I cast out poverty. I cast out shame. I cast out guilt. I cast out condemnation. I cast out lack. I cast it out of you in the mighty name of Jesus. I command faith to arise.

# CHAPTER 13

*Faith That Conquers Fear:*
## Faith vs. Fear

Fear is doubt that compromises our faith. How can we totally defeat fear?

Revelation 1:17-18 states:

And when I saw him, I fell at his feet as dead. And he laid his right hand upon me, saying unto me, Fear not; I am the first and the last: I am he that liveth, and was dead; and, behold, I am alive for evermore, Amen; and have the keys of hell and of death. (KJV)

Psalms 118:6 says, *The LORD is on my side; I will not fear: what can man do unto me?* It doesn't matter who is against you if the Lord is on your side. It doesn't matter who said "No." They cannot compete with God's "Yes."

Isaiah 54:14-15 declares:

In righteousness shalt thou be established: thou shalt be far from oppression; for thou shalt not fear: and from terror; for it shall not come near thee. Behold, they shall surely gather together, but not by me: whosoever shall gather together against thee shall fall for thy sake. (KJV)

Anything the enemy conjures up against you and any of the naysayers that are in your life, the Lord says, "Don't fear them; laugh at them because they are going to fall to the wayside."

## Fear Moves Satan, Faith Moves God

Hebrews 13:6 states, *"So that we may boldly say, The Lord is my helper, and I will not fear what man shall do unto me."* We must understand that the enemy, or Satan, cannot do anything to us unless we operate under his realm of fear. As a matter of fact, Satan can't do any more against us from fear than God can do for us from faith. As we study the gospels of Matthew, Mark, Luke, and John, Jesus always said, "Your faith has made you whole." Everything that you and I are going to receive from God is based on having faith that what He has spoken in His Word will come to pass. God is not going to operate outside of that realm of faith. He is not going to operate outside of your faith. It works the same way with Satan. He cannot operate outside of fear in your life. Every decision you make is based on faith or fear. For example, the enemy cannot control your physical body, but if he can get you to make decisions out of fear, he doesn't have to. You will do it for him. Fear moves Satan because fear is in him, and that is who he is. Faith moves God because faith is in Him, and that is who He is.

## What is Faith?

Go to Hebrews 11:1-6:

Now faith is the substance of things hoped for, the evidence of things not seen. For by it the elders obtained a good report. Through faith we understand that the worlds were framed by the word of God, so that things which are seen were not made of things which do appear. By faith Abel offered unto God a more excellent sacrifice than Cain, by which he obtained witness that he was righteous, God testifying of his gifts: and by it he being dead yet speaketh. By faith Enoch was translated that he should not see death; and was not found, because God had translated him: for before his translation he had this testimony, that he pleased God. But without faith it is impossible to please him: for he that cometh to God must believe that he is, and that he is a rewarder of them that diligently seek him. (KJV)

Faith is laying ahold of the unrealities and bringing them to reality by acting on the Word of God. You cannot obtain that which is good until you are connected with your faith. God stood out on the balconies of heaven and said, "Let there be light," and there was light. He did not say it without believing it. He had to believe it when He said it in order for it to come to pass. What you are believing God to receive has nothing to do with the senses of your flesh. Faith does not go by what you see, what you hear, what you smell, what you taste, or what you feel. It definitely does not go by what the world is telling you. It goes by what has already been established in the Word of God. Because of his faith, even when Abel's brother killed him, his blood cried out from the ground (Genesis 4:10). It doesn't matter what happens to you in this physical realm when you are operating under the realm of faith. Faith will speak even when you can't physically talk out of your mouth. You have to have faith that He *really is* God in your life.

Enoch never had a funeral. He entered the next realm. You can call it whatever you want, but I believe it. It is in the Bible. He tapped into such a level of faith that the grave had no control over his life. He walked in from this realm into the next realm, and nobody had to cry, tear up, weep, or bury him in the ground. That is the level of faith to which God calls the body of Christ. And when you think you have faith, there is another level to obtain. When you think you have arrived, there is another level to it. If you ever stop growing and getting tired

149

of hearing about faith, you have already allowed your fear to defeat you. Faith is a spiritual force. It is God's creative power. It is the substance of things desired or hoped for.

## What is Fear?

Mark 4:37-41 declares:

And there arose a great storm of wind, and the waves beat into the ship, so that it was now full. And he was in the hinder part of the ship, asleep on a pillow: and they awake him, and say unto him, Master, carest thou not that we perish? And he arose, and rebuked the wind, and said unto the sea, Peace, be still. And the wind ceased, and there was a great calm. And he said unto them, Why are ye so fearful? how is it that ye have no faith? And they feared exceedingly, and said one to another, What manner of man is this, that even the wind and the sea obey him? (KJV)

They are going through a storm and allowing their emotions to get the best of them, and Jesus is in the boat with them. Get this in your spirit. Now, the first reaction of fear is when you operate out of your emotions and start allowing your mind to make decisions based on feelings and not necessarily on facts or the Word of God. Let me say this. If you are not careful, the world will have you hiding in a bunker. There will always be another issue or another reason why you are hiding or have to do this, and everything is based on this narrative - fear. Fear of what could happen. Well, what if it doesn't happen? You have to stick with the facts. You have to fact-check the fact-checkers. And the fact is that the Word of God is the same yesterday, today, and forever. I'm not going to fear when the storm is raging, and it looks like the boat is full of water because I know who is sleeping in my boat. It is the King of Kings and the Lord of Lords.

Matthew 14:30 says: *But when he saw the wind boisterous, he was afraid; and beginning to sink, he cried, saying, Lord, save me.* He was scared. He was looking around at the circumstance. You got to be like a horse with blinders on. I'm not looking to the left or to the right. I will keep my eyes on Jesus because that is where all my help comes from. When everything is going to hell in a hand basket, I won't get in my emotions. I'm going to turn the news off. I refuse to operate and make decisions based on fear and emotions. I am going to make decisions based on the Word of God.

Fear is also a spiritual force. It is Satan's destructive power. It is the substance of things *not* desired. Fear is the opposite of faith. If faith is the substance of things hoped for and the evidence of things not seen, then fear is the substance of things *not* hoped for and the evidence of things that *are* seen. It is going by what you see instead of just shutting your eyes and saying, "God, I know you are with me. You are leading me. I'm going to shut my eyes. I'm going to grab hold of your hand. You are going to lead me and get me to the other side because if I look at it long enough, I will lose my mind." Have you ever felt like you were losing it? Your marbles were slipping by the second. You were dealing with crazy people, and you found yourself getting crazy. The next thing you know, you are all in your emotions. You are crying, upset, angry, throwing stuff, cussing like a sailor, and going crazy in your mind. Why? Because you are operating under a spiritual force called fear.

## How Does Faith Work?

Romans 10:17 says, *So then faith cometh by hearing, and hearing by the word of God.*

151

Romans 10:8-17 explains:

But what saith it? The word is nigh thee, even in thy mouth, and in thy heart: that is, the word of faith, which we preach; That if thou shalt confess with thy mouth the Lord Jesus, and shalt believe in thine heart that God hath raised him from the dead, thou shalt be saved. For with the heart man believeth unto righteousness; and with the mouth confession is made unto salvation. For the Scripture saith, Whosoever believeth on him shall not be ashamed. For there is no difference between the Jew and the Greek: for the same Lord over all is rich unto all that call upon him. For whosoever shall call upon the name of the Lord shall be saved. How then shall they call on him in whom they have not believed? and how shall they believe in him of whom they have not heard? and how shall they hear without a preacher? And how shall they preach, except they be sent? as it is written, How beautiful are the feet of them that preach the gospel of peace, and bring glad tidings of good things! But they have not all obeyed the gospel. For Esaias saith, Lord, who hath believed our report? So then faith cometh by hearing, and hearing by the word of God. (KJV)

Do you want to operate in fear? If you do, just keep watching the news. If you want to operate in fear, keep believing the report of the world. But if you want to stay in faith, you will have to keep the Word on and believe the report of the Lord. Faith is developed through meditating and acting on the Word of God. It builds your capacity. James 1:22 says, *But be ye doers of the word, and not hearers only, deceiving your own selves.* " How do you know you are deceived? You could be operating under the spirit of fear; therefore, you are buying into a lie. You have to be a doer of the Word. Faith is applied by speaking things that are not as though they were and understanding that Jesus is the author and developer of your faith. He is the Word made flesh, so the more Word you get in you, the more He will shift your life's trajectory.

## Where Does Fear Come From?

Fear comes from hearing the word of the world. Luke 21:26 says, *Men's hearts failing them for fear, and for looking after those things which are coming on the earth: for the powers of heaven shall be shaken.* Your heart will fail you if you focus on what is happening in the world. So you cannot focus on the world. Mark 4:19 says, *And the cares of this world, and the deceitfulness of riches, and the lusts of other things entering in, choke the word, and it becometh unfruitful.* The more you listen to the world, the more it chokes the Word. The more you listen to the report or fear of the world, the less fruit you produce in your life. As I have said, "Faith is now; fear also is now." Fear is developed through meditating and acting on the lies of the enemy. Fear is applied by speaking the things that are not as though they were. Fear also demands compromise. Fear will cause you to compromise on what God has spoken or instructed in His Word. You will always lose. You have to stand firm on God's Word and proclaim it faithfully. Don't read into what I am saying; read into it to what heaven is saying. Fear causes you to compromise. The enemy supports and develops fear, just as God supports and develops faith. Fear becomes doubt and unbelief when it is acted upon. Fear is not natural to a born-again believer.

## How to Cast Out Fear

John 4:15-18 declares:

Whosoever shall confess that Jesus is the Son of God, God dwelleth in him, and he in God. And we have known and believed the love that

God hath to us. God is love; and he that dwelleth in love dwelleth in God, and God in him. Herein is our love made perfect, that we may have boldness in the day of judgment: because as he is, so are we in this world. There is no fear in love; but perfect love casteth out fear: because fear hath torment. He that feareth is not made perfect in love. (KJV)

What casts out fear? The more revelation I have about God's love toward me, the less I will walk in fear and the less I will compromise, worry about, cry about, moan about, or complain about. Because I know that if God is for me, who can be against me? The enemy might come in one way, but he will flee seven different ways because the Lord will use him as a footstool. My father loves me. He has a plan for me. He has a purpose for me. If you don't receive anything else, receive the revelation that God loves you with an everlasting love. He loves you in your mess-ups. He loves you in your breakups. He loves you when you're jacked up. He loves you when you're in the pig pen. Simply put, He loves you unconditionally.

God is saying, "Get out of the mud; we are going to celebrate. I have a robe for your back. I have a ring for your finger. We are going to butcher the fattest cow in the land. You have to get up out of the mud and know that I have a plan for your life." No matter how badly you are messed up, you better get back up because God loves you, and He is going to do a great work on the inside of you and all around you. Fear not. "Fear not" is in the Bible over sixty times. I will not fear. Fear not. I will not fear. When you say it, and you get a revelation of it, the love of God begins to go to work for you. The angels begin to dispatch. God begins to move, and perfect love begins to operate. Perfect love casts fear out of your mind. When you get a hold of it, God will cast that devil out of your mind, and you will never look back. You will never fear whether God loves you or not. You will not fear whether you are unworthy because you are worthy through his blood shed at

Calvary. You will stand on the facts. These are the facts of what heaven has spoken over your life.

Fear has to be received before it can enter the heart and stop faith. So you have a split second to ask yourself who's report you will you believe? It only operates to the level or realm you receive it. When you receive it in your heart, it will begin to alter what has been established. Fear will try to undo or choke the seed of the Word in your heart. You have to resist it. The Bible says you have to resist the devil. You have to resist fear. You have to shut the door on the devil. You have to shut the door on fear. Say out loud, "No, that is not my portion. I refuse to receive fear. The devil is a liar. My portion is more than enough. By His stripes, we were healed." Resist, and it will flee from you. Mark it, "Return to sender."

## Return to Sender

We kept getting this lady's mail at our house before we built ours in Florida because she had a similar address. We had to deliver her mail. Since her house was right down the road, my wife was kind enough to take it to her. I told the mailman, "Don't bring her mail to my house. I don't want it. Take it to her house. It's just right down the street. Or, send it back to the person who sent it." Are you getting the revelation? So when the enemy sends something to you, that doesn't mean you have to receive it. You better learn to return that thing back to the pit of hell. Say with authority, "No, I'm sending it back. No, I'm sending doubt back. I'm sending unbelief back. I'm sending poverty back. I'm sending shame back. I'm sending condemnation back. I'm sending sickness back." Send it back to where it came from. Send it back! Say, "No, it can't stay here. No, you are not moving in here. Don't knock on my door again. I had a rodeo with you once, and it is not happening again." Mark it, "Return to sender."

155

## Grow Up!

The Lord said to me, "We have what we continually look at." You have whatever you keep in front of you. Proverbs 4:20 says, *My son attend to my words incline thine ear unto my sayings.* So you are going to receive whatever you keep listening to or whatever you keep looking at. In other words, if you are constantly looking at the doctor's report, constantly keeping fear in front of you, and constantly listening to the lies of the enemy, that is the report you will receive. Why does the devil keep fighting? Because he is the father of lies, and he believes his own lies. Stop listening to the father of lies. You have to keep the Word before you to see it come to pass. Stopping fear before it enters is an act of the will. It boils down to your will. It is being strong-willed.

Please don't take this the wrong way. I am not being judgmental; it is just a fact. Too many believers, who have been saved a long time, are still on milk. They are being controlled by the will of the world instead of the will of God. You can't hang out with people who are not maturing and growing in their faith. I refuse to be broke another day of my life, so I definitely will not hang out with broke folks. I will not hang out with poverty, negativity, or fear-mongering. No, you and I have to split. This relationship is over. I have the gift to say, "Goodbye." Sometimes you have to break up with people.

The problem is most of us are in love with something that can hurt us. We are listening, and it is staying in front of us. You have got to grow up. You have to get tough. Quit moaning, complaining, and griping. Get tough and get the will power to stand up and choose to believe the report of the Lord. Position yourself around people who will tell you to stop complaining and whining. You are not in a daycare; you are in discipleship. Get the bottle out of your mouth and eat some meat. Grow up so that you can pray for yourself. Mature in the Word so you can lay hands on yourself, get your family delivered, get your own marriage delivered, and get your own house delivered. Fear has not been given to you. It is something that you pick up. The Lord did not give you fear. So don't pick it up. How do we do that? We do not take the thoughts. Do not take the bait.

Luke 1:74 says, ...*That he would grant unto us, that we being delivered out of the hand of our enemies might serve him without fear.* First, He has already delivered you. *Delivered* is in the past tense. You don't have fear. You have been delivered from it. It only comes if you let it in. You have to have a strong will. You have to purpose in your heart not to believe a lie. You have to say, "No, I will not believe it. The Word is right. The word is true."

Are we Bible-believing people or not? Either we *are* or we *are not*; there is no in-between. The Word either says it, or it doesn't. "Well, I believe this." It doesn't really matter what we believe. All that matters is what the Word says. If it says it, it is final. Say out loud, "Fear, get out. Get out of my spirit. Get out of my heart. Get out of my mind." Determine that you are completely one hundred percent stepping over into faith. Get out of your emotions and totally into faith. He is going to do what He said He was going to do. He might do it in a way that you don't understand, but it doesn't change who He is. It is time to grow up, get off the bottle, chew on some meat, and get stronger-willed in your faith.

# CHAPTER 14

*Faith That Conquers Fear:*
## Don't Stop Believing

Everything is connected to our belief system. What is your belief system? How can you check it? How can you increase it?

John 20:21-30 declares:

So Jesus said to them again, "Peace to you! As the Father has sent Me, I also send you." And when He had said this, He breathed on *them,* and said to them, "Receive the Holy Spirit. If you forgive the sins of any, they are forgiven them; if you retain the *sins* of any, they are retained." Now Thomas, called the Twin, one of the twelve, was not with them when Jesus came. The other disciples therefore said to him, "We have seen the Lord." So he said to them, "Unless I see in His hands the print of the nails, and put my finger into the print of the nails, and put my hand into His side, I will not believe." And after eight days His disciples were again inside, and Thomas with them. Jesus came, the doors being shut, and stood in the midst, and said, "Peace to you!" Then He said to Thomas, "Reach your finger here, and look at My hands; and reach your hand *here,* and put *it* into My side. Do not be unbelieving, but believing." And Thomas answered and said to Him, "My Lord and my God!" Jesus said to him, "Thomas, because you have seen Me, you have believed. Blessed *are* those who have not seen and *yet* have believed." And truly Jesus did many other signs in the presence of His disciples, which are not written in this book; but

159

these are written that you may believe that Jesus is the Christ, the Son of God, and that believing you may have life in His name. (NKJV)

As believers, we need to understand that everything inside us starts with our belief system. Our belief system is crucial because what we believe affects our thinking, emotions, and feelings. It goes from our thinking and emotions to our behavior and actions. In Matthew 18:34, Jesus said to the Pharisees, …*Out of the abundance of the heart, the mouth speaketh.* He was saying that an individual's actions come from their belief system. Their mind, will, intellect, and whatever is in the heart will always work out into the atmosphere. So whatever is on the inside is a product of what has been fed from the outside. What I feed the heart will determine what I believe about the Lord, believe about myself, believe about my situation, and believe about my future. Everything is connected to our belief system.

## Doubting Thomas

In these Scriptures, we have who we call "Doubting Thomas." Jesus appeared standing before them in the room, and the disciples saw him, but Thomas was not there to witness it. To put these Scriptures in context, Jesus has risen from the dead. In the Book of Luke, we see that Mary saw Him at the tomb, and Jesus asked her why she was crying. She said, "They took His body." He replied, "Look, it's me. I am right here." The Pharisees, Sanhedrin, and Jews were not running around shouting, "He's risen! He's risen!" They were not throwing a party. They were not celebrating. It was causing a disruption in the city and everywhere. They were so mad they were ready to nail Him to the cross all over again.

The disciples were in a room; if you study this, you discover that the doors were shut. They were actually barricaded. They had barricaded themselves in the room because they were expecting a knock on the door any minute from the Jews who would tear them apart. Some believed that the disciples stole the body of Christ. There is no physical way for anybody to get in or walk into the room. So Jesus actually manifests in the room. If you read the other gospels, they thought He was a ghost. They were freaking out, but Jesus said to them, "It's me, Jesus. The one you've been rolling with the last couple of years. It's me." But Thomas was not there.

Now Thomas is there, but he is allowing what is currently going on to affect or feed his belief system and ultimately finds himself doubting someone. Thomas did not just come on the scene. He saw Jesus raise the daughter of Jairus from the dead. He saw Him raise Lazarus from the dead. He saw Him turn water into wine. He saw all these different miracles; in fact, Jesus did so many miracles that the Bible says that all the books of the world cannot contain them. Even though Thomas saw all these miracles, he allowed what he saw to affect his heart. The brutality of his experience is causing him to walk in doubt and unbelief.

How many times have we gone to a church service believing God for something and left full of faith and on fire? Then we go home and get a phone call, or something happens that doesn't go how we think it should, and suddenly we doubt God. We begin to question Him because we get tied up in our emotions and our feelings. Feelings will lie to you. You are not always going to feel it. Yes, feelings matter, but not all feelings are true. "Well, why do I feel it?" You are not asking the right question. Why do you believe it? In the book of Genesis, the serpent tells Eve, "Eat this, and you will be like God." She was already like God. She was created in His image. The truth is "you are," and the lie is "you can be." Eve allowed it to affect her belief system; she doubted the truth of being created in His image.

## God Never Changes

No matter what you are going through, God's plan for your life will never change. No matter what you are experiencing, how God feels about you and what He wants to do in your life does not change. It does not change His goodness and what He wants to do in and through you. It might look different than you thought because you believed it would happen a certain way. We put conditions and pre-conditions on how we want God to do something. "God, how are you going to do this? I want you to do it this way," or "I want you to do it that way." God will never do it the way you want Him to do it. He doesn't operate on our level. He is on a whole other level that cannot be reached. What you thought was bad, God is actually setting you up for something great. It starts with the belief system.

I am astounded by how some people believe in evil more than they do God. If you believe in it, it has power over you. I don't believe in horoscopes; where I was raised in church as a kid, that was considered witchcraft. I am not into all that new-age ideology; I stick with the Bible. It all starts with your belief system. Believe in something that never changes. Hebrews 13:8-9 declares, *Jesus Christ the same yesterday, and to day, and for ever. Be not carried about with divers and strange doctrines...* Believe in the truth. You will not fall for a lie if you believe in the truth.

## Buying In

Acts 16:31 says, *And they said, Believe on the Lord Jesus Christ, and thou shalt be saved, and thy house.* Even salvation, the baseline for receiving God, comes from believing in it. You have to believe in it. People say, "It just doesn't make sense in my head." You are talking about an infinite God! You are talking about a God who stood on the balconies of heaven and said, "Let there be light," and there was light. How can any of us wrap our minds around that? You are trying to understand something in your mind that can only be caught in your heart. This cannot really be taught; it has to be caught. It starts with believing. You have to believe it. You have to buy into it.

I am into college football, especially the recruiting side of it, so I listen to many coaches at the press conferences. They are always talking about "buying in." What they are really talking about is getting players to believe in the team, believe in the leadership, and believe in the coach. One thing I learned is that when you believe in other people's vision, callings, and assignments, what you make happen for others, God makes it happen for you. The vision of a church is to ultimately minister to people and their needs. We are ultimately called to win souls, but there has to come a point in a believer's life where they buy into the vision and duplicate what the church is doing. When you buy into something bigger than you, God will honor it by sending people to buy into what you are doing. So to do that, it takes a buy-in; it takes believing. It takes believing in the Lord beyond a shadow of a doubt. It takes believing in the vision that God has called you to do. It is hard to Pastor someone who will not buy into the vision of what God has called the church to do. They will feel out of place or empty because they are not in the will of God. It is not about you and me. It is about Him, and it is about souls. We must buy into something bigger and lay our agendas on the side. You have to buy in and believe.

## Get it on the Inside

I Timothy 4:10 states, *For therefore we both labour and suffer reproach, because we trust in the living God, who is the Saviour of all men, specially of those that believe.* So it starts with believing. You have to believe that God wants to bless your life. You must believe He

163

wants to turn your situation around for His glory. You have to believe that you can be delivered from depression, oppression, and insecurity. You have to believe that anxiety doesn't belong to you. You have to believe that you can have peace and joy. You can walk in confidence, knowing who you are, and that God has a plan for your life. People ask, "I need your help; how do I get out of this?" The first thing is to believe you can. There is a way for God to do a miracle in your marriage. There is a way for God to turn your finances around, but you have to believe without allowing what you have experienced on the outside to talk you out of what you believe on the inside. You have to get this thing on the inside of you.

Romans 10:10 says, *So then faith cometh by hearing, and hearing by the Word of God.* All this belief comes by bringing yourself under the subjection of the Word. You have to pump the Word inside you, submerging yourself in it. It is not always good to ride around with Christian music in the car; sometimes, you need to put on the Word. If it is an audio book of the Bible, get a version you understand. If King James Version is hard to understand, get the English Standard or New King James Version. I have been using the NIV because I want people to understand what I am saying. Whatever version you prefer, get it in you because that is how you will build that belief system up.

## Words of Life

When Lazarus was in the tomb, he had been dead for four days. Mary said, "If you would have been here, my brother would not have died." Jesus said, "Mary, I am the resurrection and the life, he who believes in me will live, even if he dies." She replied, "Lord, I believe he will live again in the resurrection of the last days." Jesus said, Hold up, I am not talking about the resurrection of the last days; I said if you believe, he will live again and it will be now! I want you to roll away the stone." They said, "He's been dead four days; it is going to be stinky." Resuscitation is when you die for a little bit, and they bring you back. Resurrection is when you have been dead for a couple of days, and you smell. The flesh is rotting, but when He steps on the scene and begins to speak words of life, "Lazarus, come forth." It doesn't matter if the bank, the ex-husband, or the ex-wife puts you in the tomb. It doesn't matter if you lose your job. It doesn't matter if your business is not doing as well as you want. One word from God can call you out of that tomb. She had to believe it. Jesus said, "Did I not tell you that if you believe, you will see your brother rise again."

You can tell how a person believes by listening to the words that come from their mouth. Their words tell the story. Just sit back and let people talk; they will tell you anything you want to know about their belief system. You can find out where they are and what is happening in their lives. Then you can tell them the Word of the Lord, which says, "You shall live and not die. You're the head and not the tail; you're above and not beneath. You're blessed in the city and blessed in the fields. you're blessed going in, and you're blessed going out, and everything you put your hands to is blessed." We can speak words of life into their situation. One word can resurrect them from their dead circumstance.

Did you know what you believe creates the atmosphere around you? People who visit our home talk about how peaceful it is. It is peaceful because we command it to be peaceful, even with two kids. You command! I believe peace and joy are our portions, so we carry them everywhere we go. I am not letting anybody drag me into their stuff. You can cuss, fuss, fight, and all of that. However, I'm not doing it with you. I'm not taking it home. I'm not dealing with it. I don't even believe in it; in fact, the only devil I believe in is a defeated one. You have to believe he is defeated. He was defeated at Calvary. Believe it and walk in it.

# Don't Stop Believing

John 4:42 says, *And said unto the woman, Now we believe, not because of thy saying: for we have heard him ourselves, and know that this is indeed the Christ, the Savior of the world.* What they *really* heard was the Word. Faith arose in them. John 3:18 says, *He that believeth on him is not condemned: but he that believeth not is condemned already, because he hath not believed in the name of the only begotten Son of God.* There has to be an establishment in the name, and there has to be an establishment in what the Word says about your life. You have to take it seriously and take it to heart. Do not let anything or anybody talk you out of it.

I Thessalonians 2:13 says,

For this cause also thank we God without ceasing, because, when ye received the word of God which ye heard of us, ye received it not as the word of men, but as it is in truth, the word of God, which effectually worketh also in you that believe. (KJV)

The Word works for those who believe in the Word. You have to believe in it. You have to believe that you can overcome the obstacles. You have to fight that thing tooth and nail. You have to chisel away at it, like a groundhog gnawing on a piece of wood. You have to go after it wide open and never stop believing.

Begin telling yourself in the mirror, "I am who God says I am. I am not depressed. I am full of Joy. I am full of peace. My household is peaceful. My finances are lining up with the Word." It is imperative that you start speaking it; start declaring it. You have to quit blaming everything on the devil. It is not even the devil ninety-eight percent of the time; it is just you being you. You can't sit around having a pity party. You have to keep believing. You are going to get your victory.

Blessed are those that believe without seeing. I might not see it, but I believe it. I am going to believe it with all my heart. You have to buy into this thing every single day. If you don't, someone will talk you out of your miracle. Put your seatbelt on and hold on for dear life. Blessed are those who believe. Don't stop believing!

# Faith Forward

## Part IV

# CHAPTER 15

*Faith Forward:*
## The Greatest Faith

Have you ever fasted, prayed, and done everything you could possibly do for a specific result, and yet it seemed like you did not get exactly what you wanted or how you wanted it? Then you begin to question or reevaluate what you believe and how you believe. In this series, we will learn how to move our faith forward with the most extraordinary faith.

Matthew 8:5-13 declares:

When Jesus had entered Capernaum, a centurion came to him, asking for help. "Lord," he said, "my servant lies at home paralyzed, suffering terribly." Jesus said to him, "Shall I come and heal him?" The centurion replied, "Lord, I do not deserve to have you come under my roof. But just say the word, and my servant will be healed. For I myself am a man under authority, with soldiers under me. I tell this one, 'Go,' and he goes; and that one, 'Come,' and he comes. I say to my servant, 'Do this,' and he does it." When Jesus heard this, he was amazed and said to those following him, "Truly I tell you, I have not found anyone in Israel with such great faith. I say to you that many will come from the east and the west, and will take their places at the feast with Abraham, Isaac and Jacob in the kingdom of heaven. But the subjects of the kingdom will be thrown outside, into the darkness, where there will be weeping and gnashing of teeth." Then Jesus said to the centurion, "Go! Let it be done just as you believed it would." And his servant was healed at that moment. (NIV)

Luke 7:1- 9 declares:

When Jesus had finished saying all this to the people who were listening, he entered Capernaum. There a centurion's servant, whom his master valued highly, was sick and about to die. The centurion heard of Jesus and sent some elders of the Jews to him, asking him to come and heal his servant. When they came to Jesus, they pleaded earnestly with him, "This man deserves to have you do this, because he loves our nation and has built our synagogue." So Jesus went with them. He was not far from the house when the centurion sent friends to say to him: "Lord, don't trouble yourself, for I do not deserve to have you come under my roof. That is why I did not even consider myself worthy to come to you. But say the word, and my servant will be healed. For I also am a man set under authority, having under me soldiers, and I say unto one, Go, and he goeth; and to another, Come, and he cometh; and to my servant, Do this, and he doeth it. When Jesus heard these things, he marvelled at him, and turned him about, and said unto the people that followed him, I say unto you, I have not found so great faith, no, not in Israel. (NIV)

Jesus marveled and said to his disciples, the ones who have been following His teachings and listening to His instructions, "I hadn't seen anybody with such great faith that he actually believes that I don't even have to come and lay hands on his servant, but he believes that my Word is the final authority of the result that he is believing or asking for." He is not looking for a sign in the natural. When you begin to operate with a high level of faith and move in the vision and direction that God has for your life, everything you believe God for will not be

172

there in the natural. Physical signs, feelings, emotions, or behaviors will not always be there. Understand that you cannot do it out of your feelings or what you have; you have to do it out of the realm of faith that God has already placed inside you.

## More than a Feeling

Do you feel like going to church on a Wednesday night after you worked all day? No, but you go anyway, don't you? Why? You go because you are not doing it out of feelings. You are doing it out of the realm of faith because you know it is what God has called you to do. It is the same thing with your worship and praise. Praise is not praise if you only do it when you feel like it. Worship is not worship when you only do it when you feel emotion from a song. No, that is emotionalism. And if you grow up in a charismatic or Pentecostal church for a long time, you can get more focused on what you feel instead of doing things out of faith. Faith is not giving an offering because you feel something special in the message. Faith is giving because God's Word declares that if I give, it shall be given back to me pressed down, shaken together, running over; men shall give unto my bosom. I don't praise him because he suggested it. I praise him because he commanded it. I don't worship him because I just like this new contemporary song, which feels good to me. No, I worship him because it is the highest form of prayer, and when I worship Him, He begins to move in my life. When I worship, I take the focus off of my circumstances and the situations in my life. I am saying, "Lord, it's really not about me, it's about what your Word has already declared, and I'm following through with the test no matter what is going on in my life or how I feel.

## A Needful Thing

Luke 10:42 says, *But one thing is needful: and Mary hath chosen that good part, which shall not be taken away from her.* Now let me put the tenth chapter of Luke in context. Mary, Martha, and Jesus are at the house. Mary decides that she will sit at the feet of Jesus and hear the Word or the teaching coming out of His mouth. But Martha is running around working in the kitchen and suddenly becomes jealous of Mary sitting at the feet of Jesus, hearing the Word of the Lord. Martha becomes jealous and remarks sarcastically, "Why isn't she washing the dishes? But Jesus replied, "Listen, I didn't tell you that you had to wash dishes. You could be sitting here with me. It is not about making me a meal. It is about you doing the good thing." God said that she is doing the good thing because she is listening to the Word of the Lord. She is focusing on the Word, the thing we need in our lives. Jesus called it the needful thing to sit at the feet of the Lord and hear, meditate on, and eat the Word of God. It is having faith in the Word. If you work the Word, the Word will work for you.

## Abiding in Him

John 15:7 *If ye abide in me, and my words abide in you, ye shall ask what ye will, and it shall be done unto you.* Hold on. The prerequisite to asking and getting it done is to be in the Word. If you are not in the Word, you are going to ask in amiss, and you are going to ask out of your flesh. God will not give you what you ask out of your flesh. He is going to give you what you ask out of your spirit. Often we just ramble something out of our mouth that is not out of His Word, and then we get upset if God doesn't answer it. No, we have to abide in Him and in His words. He said that His words have to be in you first. That is why it is essential that when you are working on your relationship with God, not to feed your spirit only when you go to church and hear the preacher. Get the Word on the inside of you every single day.

## Led by Feelings

This might be repetitive, but it is worth repeating. Many of the songs Christians listen to on the radio are not biblical. If you really listen to the words, it sounds like country music about Jesus. You know my coon dog died, and she left me, and I feel all alone; I feel this, and I feel that. Forget about your feelings. I want to hear songs that speak to my faith, encouraging me to get a grip on myself and move forward with what God has for my life. I'm not listening to music about my feelings all the time. If some of you were in your feelings all the time, you wouldn't even be married right now. None of us would. You cannot and should not be led by your feelings.

We live in a society where everything is about what makes you feel good. You have to feel this way or that way. Nobody can make you feel anything. You feel it because you choose to feel it. It is not about what you feel. It is about what the Word declares. Feelings destroy relationships. You have to choose to love. It is a choice. You must choose to love the Lord, your spouse, your church, and your family. They will eventually make you mad. Even the pastor will most likely make you mad. Your wife, husband, and kids will inevitably make you angry one day. My wife made me angry a few times, yes, but I still chose to love her.

## Believing Without Seeing

Romans 4:16-22 states:

Therefore it is of faith, that it might be by grace; to the end the promise might be sure to all the seed; not to that only which is of the law, but to that also which is of the faith of Abraham; who is the father of us all, (As it is written, I have made thee a father of many nations,) before him whom he believed, even God, who quickeneth the dead, and calleth those things which be not as though they were. (KJV)

You have to believe even when it looks like the opposite. Let me give you a demonstration. If I held up my Bible and asked you the color of it, you would say black because it looks black. But if God said it was red, what color would it be? It would be red even though it looks black, right? But it is black. No, it is red. It looks black, but God said it is red, so it is red. If God calls you one thing, why are you listening to what everybody else is saying? But you did this… no, no, no. You have to call those things that are not as though they are. God is not looking at how you are now. He is looking at how he designed you. He is looking at you in your purpose. He is looking at you in your calling and your assignment. And until you start calling yourself and those things that are not as though they were, according to the Word of God, you will never get to the next level of faith. You will never be able to climb the mountain and say, "The Lord brought me here, and I have confidence in His power in my life and His Word in my life, not in the words of man or in the feelings I have."

In God's sight, a person desiring a physical sign or a manifestation of something before they can believe is the lowest form of faith. It is the lowest form of faith or no faith at all.

John 20:26-29 says:

And after eight days again his disciples were within, and Thomas
with them: then came Jesus, the doors being shut, and stood in the
midst, and said, Peace be unto you. Then saith he to Thomas, Reach
hither thy finger, and behold my hands; and reach hither thy hand,
and thrust it into my side: and be not faithless, but believing. And
Thomas answered and said unto him, My LORD and my God. Jesus
saith unto him, Thomas, because thou hast seen me, thou hast
believed: blessed are they that have not seen, and yet have believed.
(KJV)

Thomas had to see something. Here is a practical example, "Lord,
when you bless me with a million dollars, I am going to give you some
money." Well, how about giving Him some out of the ten dollars you
already have? You have to start with what you have. It is not, "I am
going to do this when you do that for me." Lord, I believe that you will
do this, and then I will do that. No, you have to start where you are.
Thomas is arguing with the other disciples because he says, "Y'all ain't
seen him. Y'all crazy. He is gone. It's over. They stole his body. He is
dead. I saw him crucified. I was there." And they said, "No, I'm telling
you, He has appeared. He is alive. He is not dead. He is not in the tomb.
Thomas replied, "Well, I have to see it." Then suddenly, Jesus appears
right in the room. Thomas was looking for a natural sign.

Thomas is not the one you want to emulate regarding having faith.
He is not the "faith guy" to follow because he needs to see something
first. What would our praise and worship be like if we walked through
the door saying, "Listen, I am not worried about how I look, how I feel,
what I think, or even what is going on in my life. Blessed are those
who believe and have yet to see. I don't have to feel it because I know
God's already worked it out in my favor. There is not a devil in hell

177

that can tell me any different. I will go ahead and praise, shout, and dance like I have the victory I am believing God for."

We have to stop watching other people praise. We have to stop watching other people get blessed. We have to stop watching other people give. As a matter of fact, when that clock ticks down to zero on Sunday, I am not sitting in my chair. I am going down front because it is not about how much sleep I got and how tired I feel. That does not matter. There is a King who deserves my glory. There is a King who deserves my praise. He deserves my worship. My worship does not come out of my feelings. I am doing what God has called me to do. I am standing on the Word because I believe it regardless of how I feel. I don't need to see anything in the natural to believe it.

Luke 1:18 says, *And Zacharias said unto the angel, Whereby shall I know this? for I am an old man, and my wife well stricken in years.* He is talking out of his emotions. The Bible says that life and death are in the tongue's power. The Lord gets upset with the way Zacharias is talking. He says, "If I don't shut you up, you'll talk yourself out of your miracle. So I'm going to mute your mouth." God is so interested in blessing you with your miracle that He'll take your voice if necessary. He took his voice. He said, "I am not going to let you talk until this thing is born." Sometimes you must stop talking because your words feed your emotions, causing you to make decisions out of emotions instead of faith. And when you do that, the little fool in you comes out. He wanted a sign because Zacharias could only think about his age and body: "Look at me. Look at everything that's wrong with me." God said, "I'm not looking at what's wrong with you. I've already supernaturally blessed her womb." If we are not careful, we will disqualify ourselves because we depend on our strength to receive something. Zacharias is looking at his circumstance. Your situation can tell you that it is never going to happen. But is the Bible black or red? According to the Word of God, the most incredible faith is believing without seeing.

## Love Driven

Love makes faith work at the highest and greatest level. Galatians 5:6 says, *For in Jesus Christ neither circumcision availeth any thing, nor uncircumcision; but faith which worketh by love.* In the realm of faith, everything is pushed by how much love you are operating in. Where there is no Love… no faith, no faith… no receiving what God has for your life, it all boils down to love. The motivation behind everything has to be love. Love is not a feeling. What is love? The Bible says that God is love. So your faith in everything has to revolve around love which is completely the Lord. Everything we do has to be in love. Everything we say to each other has to be in love. Love is the essential key to having the greatest faith.

One of our pastors, Marco, and I have a working relationship where we can be brutally honest and not get upset about it. It is pretty nice because I know he loves me, and I love him. Also, I love my wife, and she loves me. She can tell me the truth. Of course, she is a little more tactful than Marco. He will just say it, but my wife is diplomatic about it. It is easier to swallow when it is wrapped in love, and it always gets things done. How often do we get in these religious attitudes and do things with no love behind them? One of the things I often pray when I wake up every day is, "Lord, allow me to be humble and keep my heart right." Pride obstructs walking in faith and love more than anything. Pride comes before the fall. Pride tears up everything. Pride gets in the way of what God wants to do and how He wants to do it because pride has to have its way. Pride is my way or the highway, not God's way.

179

Lord, don't ever let me preach just to preach, but let me preach out of a love for your people and, ultimately, a love for you. Doing it every week can become religious to you, just like anything, right? Singing can become religious to you. Going to church can become religious to you. It can be like hearing a song that you get accustomed to; it really has nothing to do with the song; it is the condition of the heart. Yet if the condition of our heart is right, we will respond the same to any song because it is about loving Him. It is about His Word and who He is to us. It is about what He has done for us and what He is going to do for us. That has to be the motivation behind it all. I am not doing this out of my feelings. I am not doing this because I am happy or sad. I am doing this because I love the Lord with all my heart, soul, and mind. I do not need a sign. I am driven by God's love for me.

Sometimes I go and preach at this unbelievable church. I am amazed how the people are so hungry for God and love the Lord so much. When I start preaching, they start shouting, jumping, and running. They are hungry for the Lord. They are not nutty, fruity, or flaky like a Granola Christian. When you talk to them after the service, you find out they really love the Lord and have faith in His word. The pastor has instilled the Word in them. Do not be moved by what you see. Do not allow fear to grip you. Do not allow any of the things happening in the world to get to you. You praise Him like you have lost your mind. You give him the glory. While you are exalting Him, He will work it all out for your good.

So moving faith forward, we are not going by our feelings. We do not worship Him only when we feel like it. We worship Him because we love Him. We will show Him with every fiber of our being that we have the faith and the capacity to receive what He wants to give us in our life. How many of you reading this can truly say, "I got it. I am going to push like I have never pushed. I am going to pray like I have never prayed. I am going to stand in faith as I have never stood in faith. I am not afraid. I am not going to listen to the narrative that is being projected by the world. I am standing on the Word of the Lord, which is to move forward, declaring His goodness in this world and in my city. That is the Word of the Lord, and I shall see my vision come to pass."

## A Prayer

God, I thank you for speaking to our hearts. Help us get out of our emotions and stop victimizing ourselves over what has happened in the past. It is a new day. We are not going to feel sorry for ourselves anymore. It doesn't matter what has happened to us in the past, it is a new day, and you have made us whole. You crowned us with Glory. We are moving forward out of our love for you and our love for others. I thank you tonight that our faith is strengthened. I thank you, Lord, that we are not looking for signs; we will praise you like we already have what we ask. We are not looking for miracles in the natural. We are praising you like miracles are popping like popcorn. We are praising you like we already have that job promotion. We are praising you like we already have that pay increase. We don't have to see it manifested in the natural to believe it. Your Word declares it. We stand on your Word and say, "We will not be moved by what we feel and what we see. You have already declared Victory from the heavens in our life, and that is enough for us to move forward." I thank you for Your supernatural favor. I thank you for the acceleration of miracles, signs, and wonders. I thank you for the acceleration of provision and favor. I thank you for the acceleration of accounts for every business owner. We receive our mind-blowing boat-sinking blessings in the name of Jesus!

# A Prophecy

I feel this in my spirit. You will throw your nets on the other side of the boat. God will give someone reading this book a miracle in two days. Look for it. You have been toiling, but at thy word, you are going to throw the net on the other side of the boat, and the miracles are going to happen. Thank Him for it right now. Praise Him like you already have it. Do you believe it? Come on, throw some shout in it. How would you respond if everything you are believing God for happened right this second? Because that is what faith does; it responds as if it has already been done. It is done! New cars are being released. New houses are being released. Contracts in businesses are being released. A raise in salaries are being released. It is done. It is done in the name of Jesus. At thy word, it shall be done.

# CHAPTER 16

*Faith Forward:*
## Real Bible Faith

Every year, most churches feel like they received a Word from the Lord concerning the following year. They use a cliché or a theme. If we are going to move forward into the things of God, we need more discipline. If you are not disciplined in the things of God, it doesn't matter what kind of theme you have. That is just Bible faith. Being a disciple is actually becoming disciplined under someone's teaching or acting on what you are taught. In Bible faith, the number one thing we need to understand is who has faith.

## Christ Identity Instead of Identity Crisis

Ephesians 2:10 says, *For we are his workmanship, created in Christ Jesus unto good works (you've been created for good works), which God hath before ordained that we should walk in them.* We must understand who we are before we can operate and flow in real Bible faith. You will never properly function in the anointing of what God has called you to do until you really know who you are and who has created you. I am concerned that in today's society, many are dealing with a severe identity crisis, not only in the world but also within the church. People do not necessarily identify with their creator to know who they are and what He has placed inside them. There are things that God has placed on the inside of you that have not yet manifested in your life.

We know that the Bible says we were created in His image. He gave us dominion over the face of the earth. We are his workmanship. God created us to do good works in the earth and to bring about His will in the earth, not our will. Not someone else's will, but to bring His will into fruition in the earth. We all have a calling and a purpose, and every person has a ministry. Every person is called into ministry, and that ministry is to do good works fulfilling the will and the purpose of God in the earth.

Understand that you are the workmanship of God. The Bible says that you were bought with a price (1 Corinthians 6:20). I deal with people all the time who feel a sense of worthlessness. They feel so "inadequate." I reply, "You shouldn't feel that way at all. In fact, your feelings are lying to you." They are lying to you because the Bible says you were bought with a price. Therefore, if you were bought with a price, you must be worth something to God. You were worth the blood shed at Calvary. That is why you have to stop letting people demean you. You have to stop letting them talk down to you. You have to stop just taking the punches and going on. Look, my mama didn't raise a weakling. The Lord didn't create you to tuck your tail between your legs and run scared. He created you as his workmanship. He bought you with a price so that you could stand up and be a voice for people who do not have one.

Faith does not work unless we know who we are. Galatians 3:22-26 states:

But the Scripture hath concluded all under sin, that the promise by faith of Jesus Christ might be given to them that believe. But before faith came, we were kept under the law, shut up unto the faith which should afterwards be revealed. Wherefore the law was our schoolmaster to bring us unto Christ, that we might be justified by faith. But after that faith is come, we are no longer under a schoolmaster. For ye are all the children of God by faith in Christ Jesus. (KJV)

Verse 22 has that f-word again, "faith." To receive the promise of faith, you have to what? Believe. Verse 26 confirms you are who? You are a child of God. It doesn't matter what Mama said. It doesn't matter what Daddy said. It doesn't matter what your employer said. It doesn't matter what the school kids said when you were young. It doesn't matter what your teacher said. You are a child of God. If you are a child of God, then you have faith on the inside of you. You do not have to say, "Oh, I don't have any faith." No, if you are a child of God, you have faith on the inside of you. It doesn't mean you are operating in faith, but you have it. Let me shed a little more light on this subject. Verse 24 says that the schoolmaster brought us unto God. The law identified the wrong in us, so we knew to accept Christ. That is how you started, but because of faith, that is not how you will end. You go from law to grace. You go from the law exposing your sin to no longer being a sinner. By faith, you have been made the righteousness of God in Christ Jesus. That is our identity in Christ. You will have an identity crisis if you do not have a Christ identity.

## Who Are You?

I have asked this question several times. Why do people sin in their lives? Because they believe they are a sinner. Whatever a man thinketh in his heart, so is he. Believing in your heart that you are an unrighteous sinner affects your thinking and emotions. It goes from your thinking and your emotions to your behavior and your actions. Jesus said, "Out of the abundance of the heart, the mouth will speak." Everything in your belief system always manifests its way into the natural realm. Whatever you believe about yourself will always come out in your behavior. If you think badly about yourself, you will believe everyone else thinks badly about you. If you think you are not going to make it, you will project that doubt into the atmosphere, and people around you will begin to confess in agreement with you. You must start believing, in your heart, that you are who God declared you to be. He said, "I have called you righteous through faith in what I have accomplished at the cross; you are no longer a sinner.

This is not just a one-time thing. The Bible says that I have been saved, I am saved, and I shall be saved. Salvation is a progression. It is a walking out. Yes, when you get saved, accept Christ, and get baptized, your spirit is born again; then, the mind has to be converted. You have to get the mind of Christ every single day. You have to nail the old belief system to the cross and allow the right belief system to be programmed on the inside of you. It takes time to convert something. Somebody said, "Well, what if I mess up and have not been converted or matured in certain areas?" That is what the blood is for. Whenever we question the blood, we say to Jesus, "Get back on the cross because the first time wasn't good enough." So you have to know who you are in Christ. Say out loud, "I am a child of God by faith in Christ Jesus."

Romans 12:3 says, *For I say, through the grace given unto me, to every man that is among you, not to think of himself more highly than he ought to think; but to think soberly, according as God hath dealt to every man the measure of faith.* It is not about you making it. It is about God making you. He has done everything. He gets all the glory. It is all by your faith, how you perceive yourself, how you perceive others, and how you perceive situations. You can perceive it by pride, or you can perceive it by faith. If you perceive it by pride, you perceive it by the flesh, but if you perceive it by faith, you are operating in the realm of the spirit. We know that if we are a child of God, we have faith.

Who has faith? Mark 11:23 says:

For verily I say unto you, That whosoever shall say unto this mountain, Be thou removed, and be thou cast into the sea; and shall not doubt in his heart, but shall believe that those things which he saith shall come to pass; he shall have whatsoever he saith. (KJV)

Last time I checked, you are a whosoever. That should make you happy to know. A revelation of that will hit your spirit and transform your life. As a child of God, you possess the ability to have faith on the inside of you, and when you speak to something, it will move in the spirit realm. Something is going to move. Something is going to happen. Something will change, but it only happens for whosoever shall say it. Who are you? You are a whosoever who believes that when they speak it, it comes to pass.

There is nothing wrong with our faith. Now, before Christ, Adam had faith, but his faith became perverted with fear. Again, what is the opposite of faith? Fear is the opposite of faith. You are either operating out of the realm of faith or fear. If you are a child of God, you trust the Lord. We do not always have to understand everything, but we do have to trust Him. Having faith doesn't mean you have to understand. Faith is following instructions when it doesn't make sense. Faith does not operate in the logical realm of your mind.

## Faith Forward

How do we move forward in faith? We have to get out of our heads and get in our hearts. We must stop letting our minds talk us out of doing big things for the Lord. How many of you have ever felt like the Lord spoke something crazy to you, and it was so big it scared you? Your mind immediately started telling you every reason why it would not work. "It won't work. No, you can't do that." Too much work, too much this, too much that, and we immediately go, "Oh, that's a lot of work, and that's a lot of pressure." Well, it is not working, and it is not pressure if you love doing it. Bishop Godair always said, "If you love what you do, you will never feel like you worked a day in your life."

Let me explain it this way. If it is from God and you truly love it, it will not feel like work. If you are operating in the realm of faith, you will not have any pressure on you. Faith will lift the pressure off of you. You didn't start it by caving into pressure, so don't allow it to get hold of you. That is in the realm of the flesh. Stay focused in faith and move forward. You may say, "God, this is big; it is massive; it looks exhausting, and it looks like it's going to take all my time. Look at my age. Look where I am. I am not young anymore," and you start rolling over. Shut your mind up and tell that thing to stop because God is not finished with you yet. The Lord is with you. He said, "I'll never leave you nor forsake you."

What color is the book again? Red, but it looks black. Why is it red? Because God said, it was red. If God says you're the head and not to tail, you might look like a tail, but you are the head according to God. I'm going to ask you again, "What color is the book? It is red because God said it was red. So, if God said you would be a millionaire, you must put your feet to your faith. You can't just wait for it to fall from the sky. Some of you think that He can only bless what you put your hands to, but it takes faith to put your hands to it. There might be some unexpected money that filters in. If that happens, it is a cherry on top, but you still have to put your hands to something, not allowing your faith to be transformed into fear. So how do we do that?

## Keep Your Eyes on Jesus

*Hebrews 12:2 declares, Looking unto Jesus the author and finisher of our faith; who for the joy that was set before him endured the cross, despising the shame, and is set down at the right hand of the throne of God.* Jesus is the source of it all. He has to be your source. There is no faith without Him. You don't have faith in your own abilities; your faith is in God. Having faith is looking to Jesus. As long as you keep your eyes on Jesus, you will not be moved by the fear. You will not be moved by the narrative of the world's way. You will not be moved by anything but faith. Keep your eyes on Jesus entirely.

Jesus was walking on water. He said, "Come to me, Peter." Peter came to Him and walked on the water, right? He walked on the water. He was looking at Jesus, but what happened when he took his eyes off Jesus? He started sinking. He started going down. Why? Because when you look around at what you are doing, taking credit and trusting your own ability instead of keeping your eyes on Him, you start sinking. "Look at this! Look at what I'm doing!" You are nothing without Jesus, but that is what pride does.

It all starts with the heart. The heart is the key. If you can keep your heart pure, you will not get offended. You will not become prideful. You will rejoice when others get blessed. Every morning when you wake up, get your eyes on Jesus. If you keep your heart right, you won't be sipping and dipping, cussing and fussing, toking and smoking, and all those other worldly things. Why? Your eyes are on Jesus. He is the author and the finisher of our faith. Stay focused on Him. Turn the volume down on the outside and turn it up on the inside. The outside will tell you this is crazy; it will never work. They will say, "No, you can't do that." But on the inside, God will prove them wrong and say, "Yes, I can."

## Get the Word in You

So how do we look unto Jesus? You have to stay in the Word. The Word and Jesus are one. He is the Word-made-flesh. We took our lead Pastor, Tina Godair, out for a birthday dinner. We were sitting at the table talking about spiritual maturity in the believer. Pastor Tina pointed out that a believer cannot merely depend on getting fed on Sunday morning and Wednesday night. Have you eaten more than once today? Do you usually eat at least two meals a day? Some of us eat more. You have to eat more than just on Sunday morning and Wednesday night. If you don't get in the Word, you will never stay focused on Jesus. Some of you just need to turn the music off and turn the Word on. Half of the music you listen to isn't biblical anyway. The Bible app is the best thing in the world because you can listen to it while driving to work. Get the Word in you while you are driving.

As a kid, we were at church Sunday morning and Sunday night. We were there an hour early because we had prayer an hour before every service. We had church on Wednesday and Thursday nights and youth on Friday nights. You just basically lived there. That is just what you did. Honestly, it made me a better person. There were times I didn't want to go, but my mom would say, "Oh yea, you going." Also, my mom made us listen to the Bible on tape. We had tapes back then. We had one of those fancy tape players that would automatically click to the back side of the tape, and you didn't have to turn it over physically. We thought we were "up there." The trailer floor was falling through, but we had a bad-to-the-bone tape player. Nobody could tell me anything.

My mom would come into my room every night and pray for me. She would lay her hand on my head and pray. I find myself doing the same thing with my son Issac. He says, "Dad, lay your hands on me and pray." And I shake him and say, "In the name of Jesus!" He laughs, giggles, and goes right to sleep. My mom would pray for me, "God touch him. Give him a clear mind, and let him sleep well. Let him have a good day at school tomorrow." Then she would hit play on that tape player. She would put a different tape in every night. Well, someone might ask, "How does that help? You are asleep; you can't hear what is being said?" While sleeping, my spirit was awake, grabbing hold of every word on that tape. I would get up and quote the Word. People would say, "How do you know the Word like that?" I didn't even know. But I know now that it was my mom playing those tapes. The Word was getting in my spirit, in my heart, and then coming out of my mouth.

That is what you have to do. You have to get the Word in you twenty-four/seven. It requires a certain discipline and a particular dedication. You don't need a word from a prophet when you have a book full of them. I'm not against a prophetic word, but you have a book filled with prophecy, your Bible. You don't have to follow the next televangelist. Listen, I love them all, and many of them are my friends, but there is a word for you in your Bible. The Word is the known will of God for you, and if we put this Word in us, it will change us more than a word coming out of someone's mouth. We have to get the Word in us. That is genuine Bible faith.

How do we look unto Jesus? Looking unto Jesus is looking unto and acting on the Word. It is not good enough to just hear it; you have to act on it. Faith acts. Faith without works is dead. So when you look unto Jesus and act on the Word, you instantly bring Jesus on the scene in every situation of your life. He shows up because He is the word. So what is believing? Believing is acting. There is no believing without acting. There is a difference between believing in your head and believing in your heart.

191

If the Word is in your heart, you will act on it. Acting on the Word makes Jesus real in your life or causes Him to manifest in everything you do.

## I Dare You

I had some friends who did crusades in Pakistan, and I am so glad the Lord never called me there. I am just glad that I'm not that kind of a missionary. I am what I call a Marriott missionary. Nope, I don't do those huts and all that. I believe God to get in a good hotel. I believe God for the money. We don't have to suffer. We just believe God for the money and stay somewhere with a nice bed and no bugs. I put my faith before I go, not just when I get there.

I have a friend living in South Africa who raised several people from the dead. It is documented. Incredible! I'd ask him, "Where did you see your greatest miracles?" He said, "I saw my greatest miracles in the most hostile environments where my faith was under fire and was being oppressed, not only spiritually, but also in the physical realm." He said, "That's when God showed up more." The Bible says in the amplified, *Dare me to see if I will not open up the windows of heaven and pour you out a blessing that you cannot even contain or receive.* He is saying, "Dare me. Put me in a position where I have to show up." That is what we need to do with our faith. Put God in a position where He has to show up. Now you have to stay open-minded about it because He might not show up the way you want Him to, but He will show up. God is showing up more now than He ever has. He is never going to stop showing up because we are always going to put a demand on our faith and dare Him to show up and do the miraculous.

## Act It Out

So believing is acting. James 1:22 says, *But be ye doers of the word, and not hearers only, deceiving your own selves.* Here is the punchline. You are only deceiving yourself when you come every week and hear the Word but never apply it. You have to put your faith out there. You have to act on it at the highest level. You have to put yourself out there like God has to do something. You have to take your thinking to another level because that is where faith is. If you can do it in your own will or your own strength, it is not faith.

I humbly say this; Bishop Godair did not ask me to come because he thought I could do it in my own strength because nobody can. He asked me because he saw the faith in my heart. To God be the glory. It takes the right heart. It takes faith on the highest level. That is the only way it will get done. That is the only way our children are going to be saved. It is the only way we are going to see the revival for which we are believing. It is not just saying it. It is doing it, saying what you mean, meaning what you say, and doing it. The head reasons or overthinks it, but the heart acts on it. So who are you? You are what the Word says you are, and you are *now*. You are not going to be; you are right now. That is why you can be the greatest Bible scholar, know all the doctrines, possess all the promises of God, and be filled with the Holy Ghost, but if you do not act on the Word, God is not being revealed in your life. He reveals Himself when you act on His Word.

Ephesians 3:20 states, *"Now unto him that is able to do exceeding abundantly above all that we ask or think, according to the power that worketh in us."* You have the power. You have the power of the Holy Ghost on the inside of you. Nothing is standing before you that God has not already given you victory over. You must believe that you have the power of the Holy Ghost right now. So stop fussing, complaining, and griping, and use the power to take control of the situation.

The gift of faith is coming to someone, and you are going to possess some things by the end of the week. You are going to receive a miracle by acting on your faith. God says, "I am going to blow your socks off and give you a boat-sinking blessing where the nets begin to break because you decided to put one foot forward and say, "God, I trust you with everything that is on the inside of me." Get ready because if you have faith to act on the Word, God has the power to bring it to pass.

# CHAPTER 17

## Faith Forward:
## Application of the God Kind of Faith

How can you apply the God kind of faith? I am not talking about the application of the human nature kind of faith; I am talking about the application of the God kind of faith.

Roman 10:6-8 declares:

But the righteousness which is of faith speaketh on this wise, Say not in thine heart, Who shall ascend into heaven? (that is, to bring Christ down from above:) Or, Who shall descend into the deep? (that is, to bring up Christ again from the dead.) But what saith it? The word is nigh thee, even in thy mouth, and in thy heart: that is, the word of faith, which we preach; (KJV)

Mark 11:23 says:

For verily I say unto you, That whosoever shall say unto this mountain, Be thou removed, and be thou cast into the sea; and shall not doubt in his heart, but shall believe that those things which he saith shall come to pass; he shall have whatsoever he saith. (KJV)

Matthew 21:21 states:

Jesus answered and said unto them, Verily I say unto you, If ye have faith, and doubt not, ye shall not only do this which is done to the fig tree, but also if ye shall say unto this mountain, Be thou removed, and be thou cast into the sea; it shall be done. (KJV)

When you are dealing with the subject of faith, everything in your life begins with your belief system. Proverbs 7:23 says, *For as he thinketh in his heart, so is he...* Whatever you think about yourself, others, your life, your past, your perspective, or your belief system will always work out from your mind to your heart to what you speak to your actions. It always works outward. Whatever is in you will always come out.

## Keep it in Line

I have this word, some people get scared about it, but it is the word *manifest*. Whatever is in you will always manifest out of you. If you are in a struggle, what you hear will manifest or activate whatever is in you. For instance, when you hear faith preached, and there is faith on the inside of you, it will cause that faith to rise and manifest. Therefore everything in your belief system has to be in line with the Word of God.

The Word was given to change the deficiency of Adam's belief system. The Word was given to transform the mind, lining it up with the Word of God. You heard me ask, "What color is it?" It is red, but it looks black. But it is red because God said it is red. Everything we do must be based on the Word and not on anything outside the Word of God. We live in the world, but we are not of the world. We cannot make any decisions or speculations or have a belief system based on anything outside God's Word. That sounds extreme. But it requires extreme belief in the Word to operate at an extreme level of faith. It requires extremism in the Word of God. Everything we believe has to be netted or entwined with the Word of God.

## Quality Time

Regarding getting the Word on the inside of you, your belief system cannot go beyond the knowledge of how much Word you know in your life. The more Word you know, the more revelation you have, and the greater your belief system is. We know that faith cometh by hearing and hearing by the Word of God. The more I hear the Word of God, the more knowledge I receive. The more knowledge I have of the Word, the more I can exercise my faith to believe God on a greater level. We have to get the Word in us constantly. To do this, we have to set routines and be consistent. We have to create good work habits and learn time management. An essential quality in a believer's life is properly managing how we spend time in the Word of God, not just on Sunday and Wednesday, but daily. While it doesn't have to be thirty minutes or an hour, it should not become a religious duty.

You can read the Word for hours and not necessarily receive anything. I will never forget the early days when I was growing up in the faith. I would read all these books about great Apostolic and Pentecostal preachers. I would read about the miracles. I would read how they would pray from 4:00 a.m. until 9:00 a.m. I automatically thought that if I wanted to get their anointing, that was what I needed to do. I would get up at 4:00 a.m. to pray and by 4:30 a.m. I was exhausted and ready to go back to sleep. I said, "Lord, I am trying to increase my anointing with all my might." He said, "Did I tell you to do that?" I said, "No, but if it worked for them, will it not work for me?" He answered, "I didn't tell you to do it." It is hard to get up at 4:00 a.m. when you go to bed at 3:30 a.m.

Every relationship is different. Some people can spend five minutes reading their devotion and get more than a person who reads ten chapters. It depends on your relationship with the Lord, not what level you are on. It is the same concerning fasting. Some people can fast a meal or two and get more revelation than those who fasted for twenty-one days. Sometimes we do things as a religious duty rather than hearing from God. Are you making progress in spending time in His Word? Are you doing whatever He asks of you? We have to get the knowledge of the Word of God in our lives. We have to spend quality time with Him.

## From the Heart

Hebrews 4:12-16 declares:

For the word of God is quick, and powerful, and sharper than any two-edged sword, piercing even to the dividing asunder of soul and spirit, and of the joints and marrow, and is a discerner of the thoughts and intents of the heart. Neither is there any creature that is not manifest in his sight: but all things are naked and opened unto the eyes of him with whom we have to do. Seeing then that we have a great high priest, that is passed into the heavens, Jesus the Son of God, let us hold fast our profession. For we have not an high priest which cannot be touched with the feeling of our infirmities; but was in all points tempted like as we are, yet without sin. Let us therefore come boldly unto the throne of grace, that we may obtain mercy, and find grace to help in time of need. (KJV)

When you get the Word in you, it is quick and powerful. It is sharper than any two-edged sword, piercing and dividing the soul and spirit, and is a discerner of the thoughts and the intentions of the heart. In other words, the Word of God always exposes the carnality that is in you. It exposes your false belief system or the unbelief that is blocking you from applying that God kind of faith.

The heart is where it really matters. Lucifer was the worship leader in heaven. He never lost his anointing. It became polluted. That is why the devil can steal, kill, and destroy people today. Do you know what changed in him? His heart changed. How do you keep your heart in check so that you can continuously operate with a high level of faith? You do it by the Word of God. When you are in the Word, you can't get offended. When you are in the Word, you are just nailing it. Call me ambitious, but you just have to keep pounding it. We never arrive. We never graduate from the School of the Spirit. It is not getting saved, baptized, and you are done. No, you keep hammering it. You keep ever increasing in the Word and your faith. As your Word grows, your faith grows. As your faith grows, it becomes big enough that whatever God wants to give you, you can fit it in. Your faith is like a basket. If your basket is too small, it is hard to put a house in it. It is hard to put a car in. It is hard to put millions of dollars in a little old basket. Somebody was joking and said, "You haven't seen my purse; I know how to get it in there."

You have to increase your faith constantly. Again, it starts with your belief system. What do you believe God wants to give you? God said to Abram, "Everywhere you look, northward, eastward, everything you can see, I will give it to you. But you have to have the ability to see it. I'll give you all the land. I'll give you the property. I'll give you the houses. I'll give it all for the kingdom of God, but can it fit in your bag? Can it fit in your faith? The only way it can fit in your faith is by increasing your faith. The only way to increase your faith is by hearing the Word of God. The Word discerns the thoughts and intentions of your heart so that we can apply an ever-increasing high level of the God kind of faith. It all comes from the heart!

## In Agreement

Matthew 10:32-33 says, *Whosoever therefore shall confess me before men, him will I confess also before my Father which is in heaven. But whosoever shall deny me before men, him will I also deny before my Father which is in heaven.* Confess does not mean you are confessing, "Jesus is Lord." The devil is going to have to do that. The word "confess" translates to "come in agreement." Whosoever shall come in agreement with me before men, I will also come in agreement with them. Remember, Jesus said, "If you have seen me, you have seen the father, for me and the father are one" (John 14:9). He wasn't talking about another person. He is everything. He says if you come into an agreement with me, I'll come into an agreement with you. All of Heaven is going to come in agreement. Something is going to explode and work out of the spirit realm into the natural realm. When we talk about your confession, we are talking about coming into agreement with the Word. Your faith will not work above your level of confession or agreement with the Word of God. Your faith can't go higher than your agreement with the Word of God.

There is a difference between the theory of what you believe and what the Word actually says. Have you ever heard somebody say, "Well, I don't believe that, I believe this? But what does the Word say? I am glad you have a belief system, but what does the Word say? If you are not careful, you will allow your carnality to develop a belief system that fits your personality rather than transforming your heart; therefore, hindering you from receiving everything that God has for your life. You have to come into agreement with what the Word says, not whatever you want to believe. It never becomes real beyond what you come into agreement with. We must come into agreement to see miracles, signs, and wonders. We have to actually believe that if the Word

200

says it, we can have it. You have to take it up another level. I will give you four actions in a formula for applying the God kind of faith.

## Say It

First, you have to say it. You must believe those things that you say will come to pass. You have to discipline your vocabulary. That is part of becoming a disciple. We have to get disciplined. Proverbs 18:7 says, *"A fool's mouth is his destruction, and his lips are the snare of his soul."* Speaking and coming into agreement is the same thing. We have to be disciplined in our communication. You must be disciplined and filter everything you say through the Word of God. Life and death are in the power of the tongue. Proverbs 18:21 says, *"Death and life are in the power of the tongue: and they that love it shall eat the fruit thereof."* Let me give you a little revelation on this Scripture. The serpent said to Eve, "You can be like God." She was already like God. She didn't eat a plum, peach, apple, pear, or grapefruit. She ate the fruit of his lips. And when she ate the fruit of his lips, she ate the lie. The lie is, "You can be." The truth is, "You already are." You will eat the fruit of whatever you are speaking. That is the fruit you produce. Do not eat the fruit of other people's lips, and make sure you are not feeding a lie to other people as well.

## Do It

Second, you have to do it. Just do it! So it is not enough to say it. You have to be a doer of the word. You can't just preach it out of your mouth and then not do it. You can't procrastinate doing it, either. Procrastination will kill your faith. It will kill it in a heartbeat. It will get in your mind and cause you to overanalyze what God has already said. When Bishop heard from the Lord, he would just do it. He didn't make any knee-jerk decisions, but when he heard from God, he did it. We have to imitate

201

him and operate in that same level of faith. Just do it. Speak it. Put a strategy plan in place and get it done. Don't overthink it because your mind will always talk you out of your greatest victory.

## Receive It

Third, you have to receive it. I say this all the time, "Lord, I receive your very best for my life. I receive provision. I receive healing. I receive protection. I receive prosperity." I say it out loud because you must say it first, then do it and then receive it. Receiving it is connected to number one, which is saying it. You have to say it and then believe it. You have to talk to yourself in the mirror. People will think you are crazy; just don't answer yourself. Talk to yourself and coach yourself. You put it out there in the spirit by saying, "I believe it." I say this often: "Money keeps on coming because the Lord keeps on bringing it in. Healing keeps on coming because the Lord keeps on bringing it in. Protection keeps on coming because the Lord keeps on bringing it in." He just keeps on bringing it in. I am confessing it and receiving it. I am confessing it and doing it. I just go about my life doing. I don't look at anything in the natural. We just do it as though it is done. We already have everything we need. We do it and receive it because we know God is faithful to perform His word. If God said He would do it, He is not a man that He should lie. He will do it.

II Corinthians 4:18 reads, *While we look not at the things which are seen, but at the things which are not seen: for the things which are seen are temporal; but the things which are not seen are eternal.*

You have to see yourself with it. You can't go by what you are seeing in the natural. You can't go by what you see in your banking account. You can't go by what your daddy called you when you were eight years old. You can't go by the abusive relationships you had in the past or what they called you and said about you. You have to go by what God said in His Word about you. "But I can't see it." It does not matter. What color is the Bible? Red! It doesn't matter what you see. You have to see yourself already owning that land. You have to see yourself operating that business. You have to see yourself with a fleet of trucks.

During Bishop's celebration of life service, I told the story about him talking about the new building. He saw the color of the walls and the seats; he even had a picture of what he wanted the front of the building to look like. He was that detailed in his vision. He saw it before it ever manifested on the property. He wasn't looking at how much money it would cost or how much money was in the bank. He just said, "This is what we are going to do." He saw and spoke what God decreed in the vision.

It is not about need. If you are only moved by need, you will be in need for the rest of your life. It will never be about need. We don't serve a God that is just about needs. Jesus said, *"I've come that you might have life, and have it more abundantly."* The word abundantly means excessiveness. God wants you to be excessively blessed. He wants you to have excess in every area of your life. You cannot be a blessing to others if you have only enough for yourself. You will always be in need. He has called you to have excess and to make a statement to the world that the church is not broke as a joke on a rope like some people think. Christians are not lazy, depressed, sad, or mad either. We are full of the joy of the Lord, and we can do things the right way without scamming people with crooked schemes. We can do things God's way and have more than the world ever dreamed about having.

## Yourself on a Shelf

Romans 13:14 says, *But put ye on the Lord Jesus Christ, and make not provision for the flesh, to fulfil the lusts thereof.* You have to put Jesus on and make no provision for the flesh. How do you make provision for the flesh? You make provision for the flesh by going by what the world says or believing the report of the world. Or, in other words, believing the opposite of everything God has established in His Word. For example, you feed the flesh by believing the negative things said about you. We must stop providing provision for the flesh if we want the Spirit of God to rise up within us. Either the flesh has to go, or He has to go. Instead, say, "I want less of me and more of Him." So we have to get less of ourselves earnestly. We must have less pride, less self-righteousness, and less anything to do with ourselves. Put yourself on a shelf. It is not about you. It is about the kingdom. He has to do it in you before He can do it through you. He has to do it in your heart. Remember, anything living is growing, and anything growing is changing. If your doubts are growing, then you are feeding them. You have to feed your faith and starve your doubts. As you feed your faith, you feed your spirit with the Word of God.

## Tell It

Fourth, you have to tell it. You have to say it, do it, receive it, and then tell it. You have to tell other people. That is why I shared the testimony about Bishop. You have to tell it. Whatever you do not celebrate will never get repeated in your life. Go tell it. Tell people what the Lord did for you. Help people. Don't be ashamed of it; don't have a false sense of humility, either. Boast in the Lord, not in yourself. Go tell it on the mountain. Revelation 12:11 says, *And they overcame him by the blood of the Lamb, and by the word of their testimony; and they loved not their lives unto the death.* Have you ever thought about just proclaiming that the Lord has already done it before you even see it manifest in the natural? "The Lord made me a millionaire." Do I have it in the natural realm? No, it is not physically in the bank yet, but that doesn't change what the Lord has declared. If He calls me blessed, then I will call myself blessed. If he calls you blessed, why don't you just tell everybody how blessed you are?

Do you know what builds a church? We can do all the marketing and spend thousands of dollars. However, what builds a church more than anything is word of mouth. Do you know how that happens? It happens because you share with people how blessed you are. They will want what you have. They will want to know why you are blessed, why you are not depressed, and why you are full of joy. They will ask, "How?" We will say, "Jesus!" They will reply, "How do I get a hold of this Jesus?" We can respond, "Go with me to church Wednesday night or Sunday morning." You just tell people. Don't hide it or be ashamed of it. Don't think people are going to label you crazy. So what if you are crazy? We all are crazy. Just accept it. People say, "You are out of your mind." No, I am not out of *my* mind. I am just out of *your* mind. If they did it to Jesus, they would do it to you. But when you are giving Him the glory, it doesn't matter what they say about you because if it is about Him, He has to take the persecution, not you. The minute you take the glory, you must also take the persecution.

When He is the one doing it, and they can call you crazy, they are really calling Jesus crazy because He is the one doing it. You can say, "I didn't do it; the Lord did it. Why are you talking to me? The Lord's the one you need to talk to. If you have a problem, talk to Him. His name is Jesus. Call Him up and tell Him what you want. He is doing it. I am just the recipient of it. I am just here with my hands lifted up and my faith high, and He continues to bless me. When I think I died and went to heaven, He just keeps on giving me more. When I think it is all finished, He just keeps on giving me more and more because He is a never-ending, more than abundant God." Tell it. Tell everyone that He wants to bless us with more than we could ever contain. You don't have to make God's word good; God makes it good. He is good, and His mercy endures forever. Go tell it!

## Shake and Move

How do you apply the God kind of faith? You say it, do it, receive it, and tell it. As you apply the faith that God has already put on the inside of you, you can watch God begin to work on your behalf. I believe that God will raise a hundred millionaires who read this book. I believe it because it has already been achieved. God can do it for everyone reading this sentence because it has already been achieved. He can do it if we will confess it, do it, receive it, and tell it. God can do it in our lives. He is willing. But we have to push it up; take it up in our faith. Apply it in our life. It is not good enough to just talk about it. It is not good enough to shuffle and shout about it. We need shakers and movers, not people that we have to put a bottle in their mouth and nurse feed for fifty years. We have to take the bottle out and give people some meat. We must say, "Okay, we have been feeding you long enough; it is time for you to pick up the slack." God is going to bless you. He is going to bless you with a business. He is going to transform your family. Get off the milk and throw the bottle out the window because you are growing up today.

Go ahead and say, "I will be a shaker and a mover. My faith is going to another level, and I am going to receive everything that God has for my life. I am going to take it to another level. I have already received the miracle, the provision, the prosperity, and the blessing in my life. I am proclaiming it in the name of Jesus." Miracles, signs, and wonders are happening as I write. You are going to another level. It is simple because the gospel is not complicated. As the Carolina Panthers say, "Keep pounding." Let's say, "Keep climbing." Keep climbing higher. Get faith focused. Get out of your emotions. Emotions will mess up your faith. Remember, emotions have nothing to do with faith. Stay focused. Say it, do it, receive it, and tell it! That is the application of the God kind of faith.

# CHAPTER 18

## *Faith Forward:*
## The Authority of the Believer

You will never fully operate in your faith until you develop confidence in who you are and the authority that you possess.

Genesis 1:26-31 declares:

Then God said, "Let us make mankind in our image, so that they may rule over the fish in the sea and the birds in the sky, over the livestock and all the wild animals, and over all the creatures that move along the ground." So God created mankind in his own image, in the image of God he created them; male and female he created them. God blessed them and said to them, "Be fruitful and increase in number; fill the earth and subdue it. Rule over the fish in the sea and the birds in the sky and over every living creature that moves on the ground." Then God said, "I give you every seed-bearing plant on the face of the whole earth and every tree that has fruit with seed in it. They will be yours for food. And to all the beasts of the earth and all the birds in the sky and all the creatures that move along the ground—everything that has the breath of life in it—I give every green plant for food." And it was so." And God saw every thing that he had made, and, behold, it was very good. And the evening and the morning were the sixth day. (KJV)

As you read the Word and study the translation from Hebrew and Greek to English, there are many things that you will never correctly understand or discover until you dig deeper on a personal level. For instance, the original translation of verse 26 does not say, Let *us* create man in *our* image. He says *I* am going to create man in *my* image. It is singular and does not mean more than one person. Verse 27 confirms, "God created man in his own image and after *his* likeness and let them have dominion." The translation changes it from Let *us* create man in our image to *I* created man in *my* own image. As a side note, He also says he created male and female, not male and male or female and female.

According to these Scriptures, whether you realize it or not, there is already a blessing on your life. You might not believe it, and you might not see it with natural eyes because you are going by what you see and not by your faith. When you get it in your spirit that God has blessed you, you will begin to walk in that blessing and operate at a higher dimension to receive everything He has for you.

## Ownership Mentality

We were created in God's image, just as Adam was. When God created Adam out of the dust, He gave Adam dominion, which is the title deed or authority to dress and keep the garden. God has given you the power or the title deed to rule and reign over every situation in your life. If something seems out of control, it is because you are not exercising the authority that has been invested in you. Have you ever felt like things are just swinging out of control?

Is there a difference between a renter mentality and an owner mentality? With an owner mentality, you see things you would not see with a renter mentality. If you had your house broken into or something stolen from you, you would feel violated because you are the owner of it. You had authority over it. It belonged to you. When you begin to operate in dominion, as God created you, and the enemy tries to take something that belongs to you, righteous anger will rise up on the inside. You would say, "No way in *H-E* double hockey sticks." You would put your foot down and say, "This is not going to happen. We are not allowing this to happen in our house. We are not allowing this to happen in our family. We are not allowing it."

You have to get that way with the enemy on every level. You must say, "Devil, you came to the wrong house this week. I'm sorry. Turn back around because I refuse to let you come into my house to kill, steal, and destroy my family. I have been given authority over you. So get out!" You have to get some Holy Ghost rage and kick him out. Ownership will always bring about a rage that will not accept the status quo but will say, "I refuse to receive anything outside of what He has already decreed in my life."

In the early part of my life, before my mom remarried, we lived in a single-wide trailer. We didn't even own the trailer, but Mom acted like we did. My oldest brother was around eighteen years old, and he was acting up. My mother said, "You are not going to act like that and live in my house because this house is a house of God." You are going to play by my rules, or you are going to hit the road." That is the kind of ownership you must have in your walk of faith.

## Excellent is Thy Name

Psalms 8:3-9 declares:

When I consider thy heavens, the work of thy fingers, the moon and the stars, which thou hast ordained; What is man, that thou art mindful of him? and the son of man, that thou visitest him? For thou hast made him a little lower than the angels, and hast crowned him with glory and honour. Thou madest him to have dominion over the works of thy hands; thou hast put all things under his feet: All sheep and oxen, yea, and the beasts of the field; The fowl of the air, and the fish of the sea, and whatsoever passeth through the paths of the seas. O Lord our Lord, how excellent is thy name in all the earth! (KJV)

When you speak the name of the Lord, it reminds the enemy of your dominion as a believer in the earth. When you open your mouth and begin to use the name of Jesus, He says, "Hold up, there is something different about this person. They are using the name which by men are saved, the name that casts out devils, the name that opens the eyes of the blind, the name that heals the sick and makes the lame walk. They use that name." If you ever get a revelation of the name of Jesus in your life, you will never accept the status quo. You will look the enemy dead in his face and say, "In the name of Jesus, I draw a line in the sand and declare that you go back to where you came from. I will fulfill the purpose and mission that God has put on my life here on this earth." You have to use the name. The authority is in His name. Your joy is in His name. Your peace is in His name. Your prosperity is in His name. Your promotion is in His name. Everything is in His name. If you keep the name coming out of your mouth, the enemy can hear it echo through the airways, and he will begin to run in the opposite direction because he knows you are carrying the name. That name above every name, the name to which every knee will bow, the name of Jesus!

## Capped Teeth

Let's talk about Adam's treason in Genesis 3:6. *And when the woman saw that the tree was good for food and a tree to be desired to make one wise, she took of the fruit thereof, and did eat, and gave also unto her husband with her; and he did eat.* Never go by what looks good to the eye. I heard a story about a pastor who brought in an evangelist from South Africa to preach because he needed someone to come in to lead a revival. He was in the States visiting. He developed a great friendship with them overtime.

The first night he preached was good. Afterward, they went out to eat, and the Pastor said, "Well, what do you think?" He said with his African accent, "Cap teeth." The Pastor said, "What?" He said, "Cap teeth." The Pastor didn't understand what he was saying. He kept repeating, "Cap teeth," and the Pastor thought to himself, "Do you need to go to the dentist?" He said, "Looks good outside, rotten inside." African Brothers don't play. They just tell you straight forward how it is. He said, "Rotten, all of them, rotten, church rotten, sin, sin, sin, rotten." The color ran out of the Pastor's face. The Pastor thought He was doing something good. He kept saying, "Rotten, everything is rotten." You can never go by what looks good to the eye.

## Fruit of the Lips

Eve saw the tree as good for food because it was pleasant to the eyes. Everything you see with your eyes can look good, like capped teeth, but rotten underneath. So you never go by what you see. You always go by the Spirit of God and by your faith. Your faith can see what is like capped teeth. The serpent comes to Eve while she is looking at the tree and says, "You can be like God if you eat of this tree." We know that starting in Genesis, they were without sin, clothed in glory. People think they were running around naked in the garden. They weren't naked. They were clothed in the glory of God. They would walk in the cool of the day with the Lord. They knew the Lord. They knew everything about Him. Remember, we read in Genesis 1:26 that He created them in His image and said it was good. So they were already like the Lord.

Eve was seeing what was good and listening to the lie. The lie was that you can be like the Lord if you eat the fruit. What she ate was not a plum, peach, pear, or apple. She was eating the fruit of his lips. The fruit of his lips was expressing a lie. The lie is that you can be like God. The truth is that you are already like God because you were created in His image. So every time you doubt you have dominion, you are eating the fruit of the lips of the enemy. You must stop eating the lie and start believing that God has already blessed you. He has already given you a measure of faith. He has already given you everything you are believing for, but you are still going by what you see. You can never go by what you see because the enemy will give you a picture of something that looks good but is actually like capped teeth. God is saying that you are trying to see it with the eye, but you will not receive it with your eye. You are going to get it by having faith. You will receive it by what I have already given you on the inside. You have to have faith in your faith.

I Timothy 2:14 says, *And Adam was not deceived, but the woman being deceived was in the transgression.* She was being deceived by her eyes. She was being deceived by what she was seeing. How do you know if you are deceived? You could be deceived and not know it because you are convinced of what you see with your eye. Have you ever had somebody give you a prophetic word, and you thought, "I don't feel like any of that was right; it is not adding up." It could be right, but you trusted what you saw, deceiving your own self. The Bible says that if you don't believe the truth, you will believe a lie. Adam and Eve fell into sin, and God stripped them of their dominion and of the power they possessed. This fast-forwards into the role of Satan.

## The Work of the Cross

Luke 4:6 says, *And the devil said unto him, All this power will I give thee, and the glory of them: for that is delivered unto me; and to whomsoever I will I give it.* He is tempting Jesus in the wilderness by offering Him power. Well, you can't offer something that you don't have. II Corinthians 4:4 says, *In whom the god of this world hath blinded the minds of them which believe not, lest the light of the glorious gospel of Christ, who is the image of God, should shine unto them.* Who was created in His image? We were. So the enemy has control of the narrative of the world. He has control of the world. He has control over it all. The only way to overcome the world is through the dominion exercised in the believer's life.

Some people do not even believe there is a devil. There cannot be good unless there is an evil to identify what is good. That is basic theology. The devil is the ruler of this world, but that rule is undone through the believers in the Earth. How did that happen? It happened through the sacrifice at Calvary. Hebrews 2:14 says, *Forasmuch then as the children are partakers of flesh and blood, he also himself likewise took part of the same; that through death he might destroy him that had the power of death, that is, the devil;* That is how dominion was restored to the believers or the children of God. It is only revealed through the light of those who are created in His image through the Gospel of Jesus Christ. Philippians 2:8 says, *And being found in fashion as a man, he humbled himself, and became obedient unto death, even the death of the cross.* So everything changed at Calvary. Everything was restored to the believer at Calvary. Everything! When He said, "It is finished," it was finished past, present, and future. It is finished. Somebody might say, "But I did this." It is finished. "But I committed this sin." It is finished.

God has already given you many chances and will continue to give you many more. The Bible says His grace is sufficient. The word *sufficient* means more than enough. Tell me when more than enough runs out. When does it run out? Does it run out at the last second when you are on your deathbed, ready to go over to the other side? It never runs out. God is not in the business of sending people to hell. The Lord is not willing that any should perish (2 Peter 3:9). Hell was never created for people. Rather, it was created for the devil and his cohorts.

John 10:18 says, *No man taketh it from me, but I lay it down of myself. I have power to lay it down, and I have power to take it again. This commandment have I received of my Father.* This Scripture is talking about the divinity of God speaking to the humanity of God. Because of what Christ had done at Calvary, you have been made a new creature, a new creation in Christ. I do not care what you did; you are made new; it is done. Nobody is holding your sin against you but yourself. The enemy keeps reminding you, attempting to hold you in bondage so that you will keep beating yourself up. When you bring it up to God, He says, "I don't remember it because I separated that sin as far as the East is from the West. I cannot help you because I do not remember it."

## The Authority of the Believer

I Timothy 3:16 says, *And without controversy great is the mystery of godliness: God was manifest in the flesh, justified in the Spirit, seen of angels, preached unto the Gentiles, believed on in the world, received up into glory.*

Hebrews 1:1-12 states:

God, who at sundry times and in divers manners spake in time past unto the fathers by the prophets, Hath in these last days spoken unto us by his Son, whom he hath appointed heir of all things, by whom also he made the worlds; Who being the brightness of his glory, and the express image of his person, and upholding all things by the word of his power, when he had by himself purged [Past, present, and future] our sins, sat down on the right hand of the Majesty on high: Being made so much better than the angels, as he hath by inheritance obtained a more excellent name than they. For unto which of the angels said he at any time, Thou art my Son, this day have I begotten thee? And again, I will be to him a Father, and he shall be to me a Son? And again, when he bringeth in the firstbegotten into the world, he saith, And let all the angels of God worship him. And of the angels he saith, Who maketh his angels spirits, and his ministers a flame of fire. But unto the Son he saith, Thy throne, O God, is for ever and ever: a sceptre of righteousness is the sceptre of thy kingdom. Thou hast loved righteousness, and hated iniquity; therefore God, even thy God, hath anointed thee with the oil of gladness above thy fellows. And, Thou, Lord, in the beginning hast laid the foundation of the earth; and the heavens are the works of thine hands: They shall perish; but thou remainest; and they all shall wax old as doth a garment; And as a vesture shalt thou fold them up, and they shall be changed: but thou art the same, and thy years shall not fail. (KJV)

Jesus gained authority over Satan's kingdom by exercising that authority through the believer. Everything is being exercised through you as a believer. He came and did it all for you. You are new. You have to believe it. You have to believe it so that you can exercise that authority. Hebrews 2:5 says, *For unto the angels hath he not put in subjection the world to come, whereof we speak.* It is all about what He has done for you. It has nothing to do with you. You would have done it long ago if you could have saved yourself. Right? If you could change yourself, you would have done it long ago. You can't do it. But when you have confidence in what He has done for you, that changes everything.

We know Genesis 1:26 states that we were created in the image of God. You know through all this, you have been created in His image. People say, "Well, what's the point of all that Scripture?" Allow me to answer that question with a question. If He is higher than all the angels, if His name is great, and He lives in you, what does that make you? The angels are actually below you. That's how much authority you have. The angels are in subjection to the God that is on the inside of you. They have to obey when you command them to stand at attention in the name of the Lord Jesus Christ. You send them, and they have to go. They are ministering spirits. They go where they are sent, and they accomplish missions going back and forth. So, if God gave you that authority, why don't you send your angels? Send your angels to go and gather your harvest.

## Predestined for Righteousness

Romans 8:29 says, *For whom he did foreknow, he also did predestinate to be conformed to the image of his Son, that he might be the firstborn among many brethren.* The Bible says that everything works together for the good of those who love Him. He has predestined us. God set you up while you were in your mother's womb. Before that, He knew when you would be conceived, and He already invested that power in you before you could even think about Him or utter one word. That is how much He cares about you. That is how much you were on His mind. Somebody said, "Well, I don't know about that predestined word. What about free will?" Well, let me explain it like this, if I put a gun to your head and say, "Choose life or death," what will you choose? You are going to choose life, right? You want to live, don't you? So you had your choice, but I still had my way in your life. God will put you in situations where you will choose His will and His plans for your life over your own fleshly desires because He loves you that much.

Remember, you are the righteousness of God. II Corinthians 5:21 says, *For he hath made him to be sin for us, who knew no sin; that we might be made the righteousness of God in him.* You are righteous. Think about the power that gives you. You might say, "But my flesh doesn't feel righteous." It is because you don't believe you are righteous. You have a sin conscious. You must get rid of your sin conscience and believe that you are righteous because the Word says you are. When you believe that you are righteous, you will begin to exercise that authority of dominion. We do not exercise our power because we do not feel worthy enough. But if He has made you righteous, you are worthy because you were bought with the price at Calvary. Stop saying, "I'm unworthy." No! You are worthy because He made you worthy. You are created in the image of Christ. You are in right standing with Him.

## A New Day

John 16:23 states, *And in that day ye shall ask me nothing. Verily, verily, I say unto you, Whatsoever ye shall ask the Father in my name, he will give it you.* Do you believe that you have the authority or the power to ask? We have His name. We have His authority and every right to use His name. We must believe that according to the Word of God, the enemy is beneath us. He is beneath your feet. God loves you. In fact, He loves you with an everlasting love. He said, "I love you enough that I will save you, make you righteous, give you ownership of the earth, and give you power over it. That is how much I love you. I will do all those things for you because I love you that much. You are the apple of my eye."

So rejoice; it is a new day for you. You might say, "Well, I didn't believe this way for so long." That is okay; you believe it now. Determine in your heart that Jesus is your Lord. Receive the Word, which is Jesus, in your heart. Confess the Word out of your mouth. Believe that your old thinking has passed away and everything has become new. Believe you were made the righteousness of God in Him. Believe that you have the power and authority to use His name. Put God first and speak His Word over every circumstance in your life. Believe that you are more than a conqueror through Christ Jesus! From this day forward, you will apply the God-kind of faith in your life. You will begin to operate in genuine Bible faith, receiving the things you desire. You will elevate your faith forward, making what looks impossible possible. It is a new day for you right now. Set your faith on fire!

Made in the USA
Monee, IL
10 December 2023